Dining In-Chicago, Vol. II

TITLES IN SERIES

Dining In-Chicago, Vol. II

A Collection of Gourmet Recipes for
Complete Meals from the Area's Finest Restaurants

**BARBARA
GRUNES**

FOREWORD BY
GEORGE L. JEWELL

Peanut Butter Publishing
Mercer Island, Washington

Cover photography by Lenore Goldberg
Illustrations by Neil Sweeney

ISBN 0-89716-108-4

CONTENTS

FOREWORD

Chicago has long outlived its stockyard reputation as the "meat and potato town," and ranks now as one of the best areas for restaurants in the world. Many restaurateurs from the Continent have established themselves here as the proprietors of establishments which feature an unlimited cuisine, appropriate to this region's diverse and sophisticated population.

Chicago has long been lauded for its innovative, award-winning architecture and its world-renowned cultural institutions such as the Lyric Opera, the Chicago Symphony Orchestra, and the Art Institute. I believe our dining establishments now mirror this standard. From my own observations I can say that more international restaurants of an astonishingly high quality have opened here in the last ten years than in almost any other city. Because of Chicago's central location and the convenience of travel today, we enjoy a greater awareness of other regional and national influences; all of these factors contribute to our city's reputation as a city of the world. Restaurants have kept pace with this development and the menus can be as creative as one is likely to encounter in New York, London, Paris, or Rome.

From my years spent in food service on the Continent, and as an Englishman by birth, I appreciate this international scope and infinite variety of Chicago suburban restaurants. I think you will enjoy the tour of these special establishments through their favorite recipes as much as I have savored my experiences dining in Chicago.

George L. Jewell

THE ÆGEAN ISLES

Dinner for Six

Egg and Lemon Soup

Cucumber with Yogurt

Broiled Fresh Sea Bass

Leg of Lamb

Spanakopita

Baklava

Wine:

Retsina

Angelos Papasteriadis, Owner and Chef

AEGEAN ISLES

As is true with many restaurants, Aegean Isles diners profit from the owner's homesickness. Born on a small island in the Aegean Sea south of Athens, Angelo Papasteriadis came to the United States in 1969 and began his career in the restaurant business. The good news for lovers of Greek food is that he eventually opened a small restaurant of his own in the Ravinia section of Highland Park.

The Aegean Isles is decorated with oil paintings of Greek towns, as well as designs by Mrs. Papasteriadis. The kitchen is visible and busy. Here, in a setting reminiscent of a small cafe in a village square, Angelo supervises the preparation of a variety of classic Greek dishes, from the familiar dolmades, gyros, and shish kebab to the more unusual Shrimp with Feta, Octopus in Vinegar, and a Mekonos Feast. "I want to present some lesser-known Greek dishes to my customers in addition to the now-familiar but still delightful mainstays of the Greek cuisine," Papasteriadis says. "Greek food, although dominated by olives, oregano, lemon juice, and garlic, provides a large array of individual tastes. The delicate licorice taste of anise is as authentic as baklava, and as pleasing, when used properly.

"In the menu, I also include family favorites such as Bougatsa, which is a fried, custard-filled pastry that was my grandmother's specialty." Looking around his domain, he observes, "Here, surrounded by the tastes and smells of my childhood, I feel at home."

561 Roger Williams Avenue
Ravinia

EGG AND LEMON SOUP

2 quarts chicken stock	Juice of 2 lemons
1 cup cooked rice	¼ teaspoon salt
4 eggs	¼ teaspoon white pepper

1. Place the chicken stock in a 3-quart pan and bring to a boil. Reduce heat, add the rice, and simmer 5 minutes.
2. Beat the eggs until foamy, then add the lemon juice. Remove 1 cup of the chicken stock and mix with the eggs; gradually stir the egg mixture back into the stock.
3. Season with salt and pepper. Serve hot.

CUCUMBER WITH YOGURT

4 cucumbers	1 tablespoon wine vinegar
1 quart unflavored yogurt	3 tablespoons chopped fresh
3 cloves garlic, minced	dill, or 1½ tablespoons
½ teaspoon salt	dried dill weed
¼ teaspoon white pepper	

Peel the cucumbers, cut in half lengthwise, and scoop out the seeds. Slice. Combine all ingredients in a glass bowl; cover and refrigerate for 30 minutes before serving.

BROILED FRESH SEA BASS

6 sea bass, cleaned and scaled, heads and tails on	⅓ teaspoon salt
½ cup olive oil	⅓ teaspoon pepper
¼ cup freshly squeezed lemon juice	1 teaspoon oregano
	1 orange, sliced
	Parsley sprigs

1. Preheat the broiler.
2. Wash and dry the fish. Combine the olive oil, lemon juice, salt, pepper, and oregano. Rub the outside of fish with the mixture.
3. Place the fish on an oiled rack and broil for 10 minutes or until tender and cooked through, basting with extra sauce and turning once during cooking.
4. Remove the fish from the broiler and place on a heated serving platter. Garnish with orange slices and parsley.

LEG OF LAMB

1 (4 to 5-pound) leg of lamb, boned	2 tablespoons salt
1 head of garlic	1 cup lemon juice, freshly squeezed
2 tablespoons pepper	2 cups water

1. Preheat oven to 350°.
2. Make several ½" cuts in the lamb. Insert garlic cloves in each cut. Sprinkle pepper and salt over the lamb.
3. Place in a roasting pan. Pour the lemon juice and water into the pan. Bake for 2 hours in preheated oven.
4. Remove the garlic cloves, slice, and serve.

SPANAKOPITA

4 pounds fresh spinach, or 3 pounds frozen spinach	1 tablespoon salt
1 yellow onion, chopped	½ tablespoon pepper
6 green onions, chopped	1 teaspoon nutmeg
¼ cup oil	1 pound feta cheese
½ cup chopped dill, fresh or dried	3 eggs, lightly beaten
	½ pound filo pastry
	¼ pound butter, melted

1. Remove the tough stems from the spinach and wash thoroughly. Steam in the water remaining on the leaves over medium heat for about 4 minutes or until limp and tender. Drain well and chop.
2. Sauté the yellow and green onions in the oil over medium-high heat until soft, stirring constantly. Add the dill, salt, pepper, and nutmeg; continue cooking until the green onions have wilted.
3. Crumble the feta cheese. Add the spinach, eggs, and crumbled cheese to the onion mixture and mix well.
4. Preheat oven to 350°.
5. Individually brush 6 sheets of filo pastry with the melted butter and place in a 9" by 13" by 2" baking pan. Add the spinach mixture and cover with 6 more buttered sheets of filo. Bake in preheated oven for 40 to 45 minutes or until the filo is crisp on top.
6. Cut into individual portions and serve hot.

As you work, keep the unused portion of the filo pastry covered with a damp towel to prevent it from drying out.

BAKLAVA

½ pound butter, melted	1 teaspoon cinnamon
1 pound filo pastry	1 pound honey
1 pound ground nuts	

1. Preheat oven to 375°.
2. Layer 3 or 4 buttered sheets of filo pastry into a 9″ by 13″ by 2″ buttered baking dish. Sprinkle one-third of the ground nuts over filo sheets. Continue alternating the buttered filo sheets and ground nuts until all the nuts have been used. Top with a few buttered filo sheets.
3. Bake in preheated oven for 45 minutes or until the baklava is crisp.
4. Dust with the cinnamon and pour the honey over the top. Score into diamond shapes. Allow to cool before serving.

Baklava tastes best cool. Almonds, pistachios and/or walnuts may be used. Baklava made with pistachios is particularly tasty.

Alouette

Dinner for Six

Salade de Canard Tiede et Salade Frisée

Soupe à l'Oignon Gratinée

Carré d'Agneau Rôti

Fonds d'Artichauts

Chestnut Mousse

Wine:

With the Salad—White Hermitage, Chante Alouette, 1976
With the Lamb Roast—Vosne-Romanée, 1973
With the Mousse—Taittinger Brut, La Française

Christian Zeiger, Owner and Chef

ALOUETTE

Alouette is the French word for skylark, the title of an ever-popular school song, and the name of a classically French restaurant in the North Shore suburb of Highwood. The menu at Alouette features items from both the traditional and the nouvelle cuisines, served in a formal atmosphere tempered by earthy tones, beamed ceilings, and textured fabrics. "Substance, rather than flash, is our goal," says owner-chef Christian Zeiger.

Christian trained as a chef in France, emigrating to the United States sixteen years ago. Here he developed his personal blend of the two great French schools of culinary philosophy and technique. "Either style of cooking can be overdone by a lack of balance," he says. "I try to obtain a happy medium. In general, I follow the principles of the newer approach. My dishes are lighter than the traditional flour-based sauces of Escoffier and the other greats of haute cuisine."

Popular entrées range from a fat-free breast of duck with green peppercorn sauce to sweetbreads sautéed with tiny shrimp and baby sweet peas. In many respects, the classical and the nouvelle traditions are in complete agreement. "We can use as much as twenty-five pounds of shallots a week," smiles Zeiger. "My restaurant is really a touch of Paris."

440 North Green Bay Road
Highwood

SALADE DE CANARD TIEDE ET SALADE FRISÉE
Warm Duck Salad with Endive, Croutons, and Bacon

6 tablespoons butter
1 duck, cut into quarters
1 clove garlic, mashed
¼ teaspoon thyme
½ pound bacon
3 tablespoons wine vinegar

Salt and pepper
1 large endive, cleaned and torn into bite-size pieces
1 tomato, cut into wedges
1 cup croutons

1. Preheat oven to 350°.
2. Melt the butter in a heavy pan over medium-high heat. Brown the duck on all sides.
3. Add the mashed garlic and thyme. Bake uncovered in preheated oven for 45 minutes. Remove the skin and slice the breast in long, thin slices. Bone the remaining meat. Keep warm.
4. Fry the bacon; remove to a dish, reserving ½ cup fat. Add the vinegar to the reserved bacon fat. Add salt and pepper to taste.
5. In a large bowl, put the endive, tomato wedges, croutons, and bacon. Toss with the warm bacon drippings. Arrange on 6 salad plates and top with the warm duck meat.

SOUPE A L'OIGNON GRATINÉE
Onion Soup

6 *large onions, thinly sliced*
4 *tablespoons butter*
3 *tablespoons vegetable oil*
2 *tablespoons all-purpose*
  flour
6 *cups BEEF STOCK*

¼ *cup vermouth*
  Salt and pepper
6 *slices French bread,*
  lightly toasted
1 *cup grated Swiss cheese*

1. Cook the onions in the butter and oil over medium heat until soft, but not browned, stirring occasionally.
2. Sprinkle the flour over the onions, stir to combine, and continue cooking over medium heat until the flour is absorbed. Stir in the beef stock and vermouth. Bring to a boil, reduce heat, and simmer for 15 to 20 minutes. Season with salt and pepper to taste.
3. Place the broiler rack in its lowest position and preheat the broiler.
4. Ladle the soup into individual crocks. Arrange a slice of toasted French bread on each. Sprinkle the cheese evenly over the bread. Place the crocks on a cookie sheet and then place under the broiler until the cheese is melted and lightly browned, about 4 minutes.

BEEF STOCK

1 *pound beef shank, cut into*
  2" pieces
1½ *pounds beef soup bones*
3 *quarts cold water*
1 *stalk celery, sliced*

1 *carrot, sliced*
1 *medium onion, sliced*
4 *sprigs parsley*
  Salt and pepper to taste

1. Place the beef, bones, and water into a large stock pot. Bring the mixture to a boil. Skim off any fat and/or scum as it rises to the surface.
2. Add the celery, carrot, onion, parsley, salt, and pepper. Reduce heat to simmer and cover the pot. Simmer for 2 hours.
3. Again skim any fat and or scum. Remove the meat and bones and strain the stock.

The stock can be frozen in small amounts for use as soup base.

CARRÉ D'AGNEAU RÔTI
Boneless Rack of Lamb

4 tablespoons butter	2 boned racks of lamb
4 large onions, finely chopped	Salt and pepper to taste
5 tablespoons sherry vinegar	1 cup VEAL STOCK

1. Preheat oven to 275°.
2. Melt the butter in a heavy, ovenproof saucepan over medium heat. Add the onions and cook until soft, stirring constantly. Do not allow to brown.
3. Transfer the onions to preheated oven; cook, stirring occasionally, for 20 minutes. Add 3 tablespoons sherry vinegar and continue to cook for another 10 minutes. Remove from the oven and keep warm; raise oven temperature to 300°.
4. Sprinkle the lamb racks with salt and pepper and sauté in an ovenproof pan over medium-high heat for 8 to 10 minutes. Turn to brown all sides.
5. Transfer the lamb to the oven for 10 minutes.
6. Remove the meat from the pan. Drain and discard the fat. Add the Veal Stock and the remaining sherry vinegar to the pan; deglaze over high heat, then reduce heat to medium and simmer 2 minutes.
7. Thinly slice the lamb and arrange on individual plates in a fan pattern. Divide the onion purée among the plates at the fans' bases. Spoon the pan sauce over the meat and serve.

VEAL STOCK

2 pounds veal knuckles	1 medium-size onion, chopped
4 peppercorns	2 stalks celery, chopped
1 bay leaf	1 carrot, sliced
3 sprigs parsley	

1. Place the veal knuckles in at least 4 quarts cold water and slowly bring to a boil. Remove from heat and drain; discard the water.
2. Place the blanched veal in a 4-quart stock pot with 2 quarts fresh water and the remaining ingredients. Bring to a boil. Reduce heat and simmer at least 2½ hours, skimming off any scum as it rises to the surface.
3. Strain the stock, allow to cool, and refrigerate. Remove the solidified fat from the top before using.

Makes 1 quart stock.

FONDS D'ARTICHAUTS
Artichoke Bottoms

6 *large artichokes*	3 *tablespoons olive oil*
1¼ *cups water*	½ *teaspoon salt*
½ *cup white wine*	¼ *teaspoon pepper*
½ *large onion, thinly sliced*	2 *bay leaves*
1 *small lemon, thinly sliced*	½ *head romaine lettuce*

1. Remove all the leaves and the fuzzy 'chokes' from the artichokes. Remove the stems and peel away any tough skin left on the bottoms. Quarter the bottoms.
2. Combine the artichoke bottoms and the remaining ingredients except the lettuce in a saucepan. Bring to a boil, reduce heat, and simmer 15 minutes. Transfer with the liquid to a glass bowl and allow to cool.
3. Wash and dry the lettuce and tear into bite-size pieces. Divide onto individual salad plates.
4. Spoon the artichoke bottoms over the lettuce and serve.

The liquid in which the artichoke bottoms are cooked serves as a dressing for the lettuce in this recipe.

ALOUETTE

CHESTNUT MOUSSE

4 egg yolks
¾ cup sugar
1 pint milk, scalded and
  cooled to room temperature
1 package unflavored gelatin
¼ cup cold water

1 (15½-ounce) can
  chestnut purée
½ pint whipping cream,
  chilled
3 egg whites, room
  temperature

1. Beat egg yolks and ¼ cup of the sugar until light.
2. Place the egg mixture in the top part of a double boiler. Mix in the cooled milk. Cook, stirring constantly, over medium heat until the mixture thickens and will coat a spoon.
3. Sprinkle the gelatin over the cold water to dissolve. Stir gelatin into the custard. Cool until it begins to set.
4. Place the chestnut purée in a bowl. Mash with a fork until smooth, then mix into the custard.
5. Whip the cream until it holds a shape. Fold into the custard mixture.
6. Beat the egg whites until stiff peaks form. Heat the remaining sugar in a small saucepan to 240°. Mix the sugar into the egg whites in a slow, steady stream until combined. Fold the egg whites into the custard.
7. Spoon the mixture into a soufflé dish or other large container. Cover and refrigerate until set, about four to six hours. Spoon into dessert dishes at the table.

La Bohème

Dinner for Six

Lotte en Papillote

Spinach Salad

Broiled Tomatoes

Escalopes de Veau Normande

Tarte Tatin

Wine:
Sylvaner

Jacques Barbier, Owner and Chef

LA BOHÈME

Transporting the ambiance of Normandy across the Atlantic Ocean is no simple task but it is a task that Jacques Barbier relishes and accomplishes with ease at La Bohème. Situated in the heart of Winnetka, the restaurant evokes the half-timbered inns that dot the Norman countryside. The warm atmosphere is developed by a fireplace, large windows overlooking a courtyard, and copper pots and plates hung artistically on the walls. Brick floors and several posters depicting the historic Norman city of Rouen, with its famous clock, complete the setting.

Then there is the cuisine. "First," explains Jacques, "I have tried to be faithful to the foods of my native Rouen. In addition, we cook frequently with cream and apples, as they do on the coast of northern France. In Normandy we lean toward fish as a staple in the diet because we are so close to the sea. Mussels, sea scallops, and most fish are elements in my menu here just as they were at home."

Patrons are invited to bring their own favorite wines to accompany the wide selection of French provincial foods, as well as an array of desserts ranging from genoise to profiteroles. "I want my guests to leave with sweet memories," smiles Chef Barbier, "and what could accomplish that better than the perfection of French pastry?"

566 Chestnut
Winnetka

LA BOHÈME

LOTTE IN PAPILLOTE

3 tomatoes	Salt to taste
1½ pounds filet of lotte (monkfish or anglerfish)	Freshly ground black pepper to taste
Olive oil	Oil for deep-frying
6 slices cooked ham	
6 tablespoons DUXELLES (see next page)	

1. Slice the tomatoes to produce about 6 slices each. Arrange on a baking sheet and place under a hot broiler for about 2 minutes or until cooked. Remove and set aside; turn the oven down to 400°.
2. Cut 6 pieces of parchment paper into heart shapes about 8″ across. Cut the fish filet into 6 portions.
3. For each serving, oil one side of a parchment heart. Spread one side of a ham slice with 1 tablespoon Duxelles and lay a portion of the fish on this side. Roll the fish up in the ham and place on one lobe of the heart. Top with 3 broiled tomato slices and season with salt and pepper. Fold the other lobe of the heart over to enclose; seal the edges securely with a double fold all the way around. Repeat the process for the remaining portions.
4. Heat about 1½″ of cooking oil in a large, deep skillet. Place the wrapped fish in the hot oil. When the papillotes—the fish packages—begin to puff out, transfer to a baking pan and place in the preheated oven for 4 minutes more.
5. Remove and place on individual plates. Serve as is—*en papillote.*

Lotte is known in France as 'the poor man's lobster'.

LA BOHÈME

DUXELLES

12 large mushrooms
6 large shallots
6 tablespoons butter
 BOUQUET GARNI
 Salt to taste

Freshly ground black
pepper to taste
¼ cup crème fraîche (see note)
 or whipping cream

1. Wipe the mushrooms clean with a damp towel. Mince as finely as it is possible to do with a knife—do not use a meat chopper or a blender.
2. Put the minced mushrooms in a kitchen towel and twist the towel to press out as much moisture as possible.
3. Finely mince the shallots. Heat 5 tablespoons butter in a casserole or saucepan. Add the shallots and cook, stiring constantly, until soft.
4. Add the remaining 1 tablespoon butter and the mushrooms, stirring with a wooden spoon. Add the Bouquet Garni, salt, and pepper and simmer over low heat until all the pan liquid has evaporated.
5. Remove from heat, remove the Bouquet Garni and stir in the crème fraîche.

Note: Crème fraiche may be purchased at specialty dairies, or it may be made at home: Add ½ cup sour cream to 1 cup whipping cream, both tepid, and stir gently but thoroughly. Leave at room temperature overnight in a covered jar, then stir well and refrigerate until ready to use. In addition to its occasional use in French cooking, it is excellent over fresh fruit.

Extra Duxelles may be refrigerated for use as a condiment or, with the addition of a little chopped parsley, as a garnish for small cuts of meat.

BOUQUET GARNI

1 sprig parsley
2 sprigs thyme

1 bay leaf
1 sprig marjoram (optional)

Tie with string in a small bouquet.

If herb sprigs are not available, chopped or rubbed herbs may be used. In that case, tie in a small square of cheesecloth.

SPINACH SALAD

1 *pound fresh spinach*	3 *ounces olive oil*
1 *teaspoon sugar*	3 *ounces lemon juice*
¼ *teaspoon salt*	2 *hard-cooked eggs,*
¼ *teaspoon freshly ground*	*finely chopped*
pepper	12 *mushrooms, sliced*
¼ *teaspoon dry mustard*	½ *cup flavored croutons*

1. Wash thoroughly , dry, and shred the spinach. Place in a deep bowl and set aside.
2. Combine the sugar, salt, pepper, mustard, olive oil, and lemon juice.
3. Toss the dressing with the shredded spinach. Mix in the egg and mushrooms.
4. Divide the salad onto 6 chilled salad plates. Sprinkle the croutons over.

BROILED TOMATOES

6 *medium-size firm*	1 *teaspoon minced*
tomatoes, trimmed	*fresh basil*
3 *tablespoons butter*	½ *teaspoon salt*
½ *cup bread crumbs*	¼ *teaspoon pepper*

1. Cut the tomatoes in half crosswise and arrange in a lightly buttered pan.
2. Heat the butter in a small skillet. Sauté the bread crumbs with the basil, salt, and pepper until the butter is absorbed.
3. Sprinkle the seasoned crumbs over the tomatoes. Place 6″ to 7″ below a hot broiler for 4 minutes. Serve 2 halves per person.

LA BOHÈME

ESCALOPES DE VEAU NORMANDE

1½ pounds veal, cut from the upper leg	½ cup sliced mushrooms
¼ cup peanut oil	2 cups crème fraîche
7 tablespoons butter	Salt
Flour for dredging	Freshly ground black pepper
½ cup Calvados	2 cups sliced apple
	¼ cup minced parsley

1. Cut the veal into 2-ounce chunks. With a meat mallet, pound each piece on both sides until thin and flat.
2. Heat the oil and 4 tablespoons of the butter in a deep skillet over medium-high heat. Dredge the veal in flour and sauté quickly until golden on both sides. Transfer to a serving dish and keep warm.
3. Pour off the fat from the veal pan. Add the Calvados and flame over high heat, lighting with a match if necessary. Add the sliced mushrooms and crème fraîche and immediately reduce heat to simmer. Cook gently until the sauce reduces almost to the consistency of sour cream. Season to taste with salt and pepper; keep warm.
4. In a separate pan, melt the remaining 3 tablespoons butter over medium heat. Add the sliced apple and sauté until soft.
5. To serve, pour the mushroom sauce over the veal slices and top with the sautéed apple. Sprinkle with minced parsley and serve very hot.

This recipe is from the rocky shores of Normandy, a land of apples, superb creamery goods, and people with a love of good food. Calvados is a fine brandy made from the apples of Normandy.

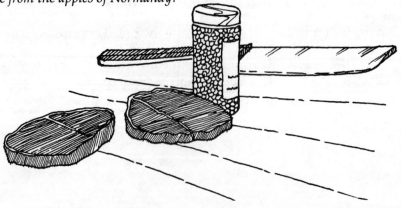

TARTE TATIN

FLAKY PASTRY DOUGH
½ cup butter

1¼ cups granulated sugar
2¾ pounds cooking apples

1. Preheat oven to 400°.
2. On a floured table, roll out the dough ¹⁄₁₆" thick in an 11" circle. Place on a plate and prick with a fork. Refrigerate while you prepare the apples.
3. Melt the butter and sugar over low heat in a deep 10" pie pan. Peel, core, and slice the cooking apples. Place in the pie pan very close together, and continue cooking very slowly until the sugar begins to caramelize. This should take about 10 minutes, and the apples should soften considerably. The caramel should be very light in color.
4. Place the pan in the preheated oven for 5 minutes. Remove and cover the apples with the rolled-out dough, crimping the edges to the pan to seal in the caramelized apples. Raise the oven temperature to 450° and continue baking for 20 minutes or until the crust looks done.
5. Invert the tart onto a serving platter. Serve warm.

This recipe was developed and immortalized by the sisters Tartin of France at their inn.

A deep-crusted pizza pan reserved solely for making tarte tatin works very well.

FLAKY PASTRY DOUGH

1¼ cups all-purpose flour
¼ teaspoon salt
4 tablespoons butter, room temperature

3 tablespoons vegetable shortening, room temperature
5 to 7 tablespoons ice water

1. Combine the flour and salt in a large mixing bowl.
2. Cut the butter and vegetable shortening into the flour with 2 knives or a pastry knife, or use a food processor fitted with a steel blade. Mix in the ice water with a wooden spoon until the dough forms a ball.
3. Turn out onto a lightly floured board and knead 1 minute. Cover with plastic wrap and refrigerate for 1 hour.

Café Provençal

Dinner for Six

Piments Doux et Anchois Italiennes

Soupe au Safran

Caneton Rôti aux Figues

Fevettes à la Verdure

Tarte au Citron, Sauce Myrtille

Wine:

With the Piments Doux and Soup—Mâcon-Villages Blanc, Jadot, 1979

With the Caneton Rôti—Marcilly Reserve, 1971

*With the Tarte—Château St. Jean Johannisberg Riesling,
late harvest, Belle Terre*

Leslee Reis, Owner and Chef

CAFÉ PROVENÇAL

The simple sophistication and warmth that is so typical of the French countryside dominates both the atmosphere and the cuisine of the Café Provençal in Evanston. "I wanted to bring French country food to the Chicago area," says Leslee Reis, chef-owner.

Leslee was trained at the Cordon Bleu school of cooking in Paris. Although she has an advanced degree from Harvard University in the field of biochemistry, her growing interest in food led her to develop a catering business which eventually blossomed into this charming restaurant.

Café Provençal has a natural feeling, enhanced by warm woods and a large fireplace. On the southern wall is a garden room with an outdoor view. The main room of the Café Provençal is dominated by a pink floral painting, commissioned by Leslee after the restaurant was opened. Looking around the room one sees the elegant Villeroy and Boch china, pink tablecloths, fresh flowers, and soft print.

The scientist's passion for research and development remains evident in Leslee's continually changing menus. "My choice of daily offerings depends on the time of year and varies with the availability of seasonal produce, although I always emphasize fresh fish," Leslee explains. "I always maintain an herb garden just outside the kitchen door, just as the rural housewife does. This allows me spontaneous creativity with fresh seasonings."

1625 Hinman Avenue
Evanston

PIMENTS DOUX ET ANCHOIS ITALIENNE

4 bell peppers, red or green
1 (2-ounce) can anchovy
  filets
  Salt and pepper
  Oregano

3 cloves garlic, crushed
3 tablespoons capers
1 tablespoon chopped parsley
¼ cup olive oil
  French bread

1. Char the peppers under a broiler, turning frequently, until all sides are blistered. Peel while still hot. Remove the seeds and soft pulp inside. Slice lengthwise into strips about 1" to 1½" wide.
2. Lay one-third of the sliced peppers in a serving dish. Place a third of the anchovies atop. Season lightly with salt, pepper, and oregano. Sprinkle one-third of the crushed garlic, 1 tablespoon capers, and 1 teaspoon parsley over. Repeat for 2 more layers.
3. Add olive oil to coat. Marinate for several hours before serving with French bread.

I prefer a French olive oil, such as James Plagniol.

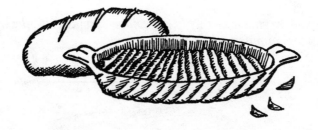

CAFÉ PROVENÇAL

SOUPE AU SAFRAN

5 tablespoons butter	White pepper
2 leeks, whites only, thinly sliced	5½ cups CHICKEN STOCK (see next page)
1 carrot, thinly sliced	¾ teaspoon saffron, or to taste
2 medium-size baking potatoes, peeled and sliced	½ cup CRÈME FRAÎCHE (see next page)
Salt	

1. Melt the butter in a 2 or 3-quart saucepan over medium heat. Sauté the leeks, covered, for about 5 minutes or until softened.
2. Add the carrot and potatoes. Season to taste with salt and white pepper. Cover and simmer over very low heat, stirring frequently, for 25 to 30 minutes. Do not allow to burn.
3. Add 5 cups Chicken Stock. Return to a boil, cover, reduce heat, and simmer 30 minutes more.
4. Purée in a blender or food processor.
5. Place ½ teaspoon saffron threads in a cup. Pour ½ cup boiling Chicken Stock over; allow to steep at least 5 minutes.
6. Stir the saffron stock and Crème Fraîche into the puréed soup. Taste for seasoning and adjust if needed. Garnish with the remaining saffron threads and serve.

The dried stigmas of the crocus flower constitute the saffron spice. Saffron has been used since remote antiquity as a condiment, a medicinal herb, and a textile dye.

This soup may be enjoyed either hot or cold; if serving cold, the seasonings will need to be more pronounced.

CHICKEN STOCK

5 pounds chicken, cut in pieces	5 sprigs parsley
½ pound chicken gizzards	2 carrots, sliced
4 stalks celery, sliced	2 teaspoons salt

1. Place all ingredients except the salt in an 8-quart pot. Add cold water to cover. Bring to a boil over medium-low heat.
2. Skim off the foam that rises to the top. Add the salt, cover tightly, reduce heat, and simmer 1 hour.
3. Taste for seasoning and adjust if necessary. Continue simmering for 1½ hours.
4. Remove the chicken pieces from the stock. Strain through 2 layers of cheesecloth, allow to cool, and refrigerate. Before using, remove the layer of solidified fat that has accumulated on top.

Makes about 6 cups stock.

CRÈME FRAÎCHE

1 cup whipping cream	1 tablespoon sour cream or buttermilk

1. Heat the cream to 90°, or cool-lukewarm. Stir in the sour cream or buttermilk. Cover and allow to stand at room temperature for 8 to 12 hours, or until the mixture begins to thicken.
2. Refrigerate at least 24 hours before using.

Crème Fraîche should be thickened almost to the spreadable consistency of sour cream. This recipe makes 1 cup.

CANETON RÔTI AUX FIGUES

2 (4-pound) Long Island ducklings
⅓ cup chopped celery
⅓ cup chopped onion
⅓ cup chopped carrots
⅓ cup chopped parsley
2 cups Chicken Stock (see Soupe au Safran recipe)
½ lemon
Salt

Pepper
2 tablespoons sugar
½ cup burgundy
½ teaspoon dried thyme, or 2 sprigs fresh thyme
12 fresh figs, or 1 pound dried figs
Watercress sprigs for garnish

1. Pull the fat from the duck cavities and reserve. Remove the tips and second joints from the wings and reserve. Quarter the gizzards.
2. Render the duck fat in a 2-quart saucepan over medium-high heat. Add the wing pieces, quartered gizzards, and necks and brown about 10 minutes.
3. Add the celery, onion, carrots, and parsley. Cook 5 to 10 minutes, stirring frequently.
4. Drain off the fat and discard. Add the chicken stock and bring to a rapid boil. Stir, reduce heat, and simmer about 1½ hours.
5. Preheat oven to 500°. Rub the duck cavities with the lemon half. Sprinkle salt and pepper inside and out. Roast on a rack in preheated oven for 20 minutes. Drain off fat, reduce oven temperature to 400°, and roast an additional 40 to 60 minutes until the meat is cooked and tender and the juices run clear, pouring off fat as it accumulates during roasting. Remove the ducks from the pan; cover to keep warm and set aside. Drain the fat from the pan, but reserve the cracklings.
6. In a separate pan, dissolve the sugar in the red wine. Add the thyme and figs. Simmer 5 minutes for fresh figs, or 45 minutes for dried, adding water as necessary to keep covered. Remove the figs (and sprigs of thyme, if using). Over high heat, reduce the pan liquid to a light syrup. Cut off the tops of the figs so they open like flower buds. Place in a bowl and pour the syrup over. Keep covered.
7. Strain the duck stock into the roasting pan with the cracklings. Place over medium heat and bring to a boil while scraping the cracklings to dissolve. Reduce heat and simmer until the volume is reduced by one-third. Add salt and pepper to taste.

8. Return the figs in syrup to low heat and warm slowly. Drain the syrup into the duck stock, cooking until the flavors blend. Adjust seasoning if necessary.
9. Place the ducks on a platter. Surround with the figs, ladle the sauce over, and garnish with watercress sprigs.

FÉVETTES A LA VERDURE

1 pound fresh or frozen lima beans	1 teaspoon thyme, or several sprigs fresh thyme
½ cup water	Salt and pepper to taste
1 large head Boston lettuce, cut in chiffonade	1 to 2 tablespoons olive oil or butter
½ cup chopped green onions	

1. Wash the beans if fresh, or partially thaw if frozen. Place in a saucepan with the water, lettuce, green onions, and seasonings. Bring to a boil and cook uncovered over medium heat until tender—10 to 30 minutes, depending on size and whether fresh or frozen. Add more water, a little at a time, if necessary during cooking. There should be no water left in the pan at the finish.
2. Add the olive oil or butter and stir in well. Taste for seasoning and correct if necessary.

'Chiffonade' means finely sliced strips. For lettuce, this is generally almost a julienne.

TARTE AU CITRON, SAUCE MYRTILLE

PÂTE BRISÉE
Zest and juice of 3 large
lemons
¾ cup sugar
7 egg yolks

3 whole eggs
1 teaspoon gelatin
1 tablespoon water
¼ cup butter, softened
SAUCE MYRTILLE (see
next page)

1. Roll the Pâte Brisée into a circle about 11" in diameter on a lightly floured board. Press into an 8" or 9" flan ring. Trim the edges and prick holes in the bottom with a fork. Bake at 425° for 5 minutes. Cover with aluminum foil, fill with dried beans, and continue baking for 10 to 15 minutes or until the crust is lightly browned. Remove the beans and foil and bake 2 minutes longer. Cool 10 minutes.
2. In the top part of a double boiler, place the lemon zest and juice, sugar, egg yolks, and whole eggs. Cook, whisking constantly, over barely simmering water until fairly thick—about 15 to 20 minutes. Remove from heat.
3. Place the gelatin and water over low heat until the gelatin is thoroughly dissolved. Stir into the lemon/egg mixture. Whisk in the softened butter until thoroughly blended.
4. Fill the crust with the egg mixture. Allow to cool 2 hours.
5. Slice the tart into serving portions. Just before serving, spoon a generous amount of Sauce Myrtille over each portion.

PÂTE BRISÉE

2¼ cups all-purpose flour
3 tablespoons sugar
¼ teaspoon salt
7 tablespoons butter, room
temperature

3 tablespoons vegetable
shortening, room
temperature
2 egg yolks
½ cup less 1 tablespoon
ice water

1. Combine the flour, sugar, and salt in a large mixing bowl. Cut in the butter and shortening until the mixture has the texture of coarse meal.
2. Mix in the egg yolks and ice water, stirring with a wooden spoon until the dough forms a ball. Cover with plastic wrap and chill 1 hour before using.

SAUCE MYRTILLE

1 pint fresh blueberries
¼ cup sugar

2 tablespoons kirsch or brandy

Combine the ingredients and stir well. Allow to sit in the refrigerator at least 1 hour before using.

"The Cottage"

Dinner for Six

Smoked Lake Troute Pâté

Cream of Sorrel Soup

Cottage Schnitzel

Bibb Lettuce with Celery Vinaigrette Dressing

Raspberry Cake

Wine:

Kendermann Liebfraumilch, 1979
or
Robert Mondavi Chenin Blanc, 1980

Carolyn and Jerry Buster, Owners

Carolyn Buster, Chef

THE COTTAGE

In the eight years since they opened the Cottage in south-suburban Calumet City, Carolyn and Jerry Buster have striven to serve sophisticated Continental cuisine in an atmosphere conducive to its enjoyment. White linen tablecloths, cushioned chairs, fresh flowers, and antique silver throughout the intimate, wood beamed dining room establish a tone of elegant ease.

But the air of relaxation ends abruptly when you enter the kitchen. Here, Carolyn Buster, chef's hat perched on her head, works continuously to turn out the ever-changing menu. "Although I lean slightly toward the French style, as a result partly of my Cordon Bleu training and partly, of course, because of its dominance in the cooking world, I try to incorporate ideas and tastes from all over Europe in my menus," she says. "Furthermore, I don't feel bound by tradition—only inspired by it." One example of this philosophy is the popular Cottage Schnitzel. Here, the usual veal is successfully replaced by thin pork medallions that are lightly battered, sautéed, and served in a lemony butter sauce.

Mirroring this theme of individuality informed by tradition, Jerry Buster supervises an eclectic wine cellar. "I choose the wines we stock with the same eye to excellence that Carolyn uses in the kitchen," Jerry comments. "Even though we lean heavily toward the California vintages, because of their popularity and quality, we try to include in our selection samples from many areas of the world. It is important for us to feel that we have brought the best possible food, service, and wine to our guests."

525 Torrence Avenue
Calument City

SMOKED LAKE TROUT PÂTÉ

1 *pound smoked lake trout*
½ *Granny Smith apple, cored*
1½ *tablespoons hot horseradish, or to taste*
1 *teaspoon lemon juice*
3 *green onions, finely chopped*

½ *teaspoon ground white pepper*
¼ *teaspoon garlic powder*
½ *teaspoon salt*
Zest of 1 small orange

1. Filet the trout, removing the skin and all bones.
2. Chop the apple fairly finely and mix with the horseradish and lemon juice, or put all 3 ingredients in a food processor fitted with a steel blade and process until the apple is medium-fine.
3. Finely chop the green onions with a knife. Combine with the apple mixture.
4. Place the fish, pepper, garlic, and salt in a food processor and process until well blended, or run twice through a food grinder. Remove to a bowl and fold in the apple mixture.
5. Mince the orange zest and fold into the pâté.

CREAM OF SORREL SOUP

¼ pound butter
½ cup minced onion
¼ cup diced carrot
1 large boiling potato, peeled and diced
1 bay leaf
¼ cup chopped parsley
Salt and white pepper to taste

Garlic powder to taste
1 quart CHICKEN STOCK (see next page)
2 tablespoons flour
2 tablespoons cornstarch
1 cup half-and-half
1 cup sorrel, fresh or packed in water
1 pint sour cream

1. Melt the butter in a heavy stock pot over medium-high heat. Add the onion, carrot, potato, bay leaf, parsley, salt, pepper, and garlic powder and sauté until the vegetables begin to soften. Do not brown.
2. Add the stock, bring to a boil, reduce heat, and simmer 20 minutes or until the potatoes are tender.
3. Return the soup to a rolling boil and remove from heat. Mix the flour and the cornstarch. Stir the half-and-half in slowly, whisking the mixture to dissolve all lumps. Whisk slowly into the hot soup.
4. If using fresh sorrel, strip the mid-ribs from the leaves and discard. Immerse for 1 minute in 1 gallon boiling salted water; drain. If using canned sorrel, merely drain. Shred the sorrel.
5. Skim 2 cups stock from the soup and place in a blender or food processor with the shredded sorrel; purée.
6. In a bowl, combine the puréed sorrel and sour cream. Skim another ½ cup stock and blend in, then blend the sorrel mixture back into the soup. Serve hot.

I recommend Le Semeur brand sorrel if fresh sorrel isn't available.

CHICKEN STOCK

1 pound chicken wings and backs	1½ teaspoons salt
5 cups water	3 peppercorns
1½ stalks celery, chopped	3 sprigs parsley
1 small onion, chopped	1 small turnip, chopped
	2 carrots, chopped

Place all ingredients in a stock pot. Bring to a boil, reduce heat, and simmer 2 hours. Strain before using.

COTTAGE SCHNITZEL

2 pounds pork tenderloin thoroughly trimmed	½ teaspoon salt
2 large eggs	¼ teaspoon white pepper
2 tablespoons flour, plus more for dredging	Pinch of nutmeg
2 tablespoons grated Parmesan cheese	1 tablespoon freshly chopped parsley
½ cup milk	6 tablespoons butter
	2 tablespoons fresh lemon juice

1. Slice the tenderloins ¼" thick. Flatten slightly with a meat mallet or the flat side of a cleaver. The medallions should be about 3" across.
2. Lightly beat the eggs. Add the 2 tablespoons flour and beat to combine. Add the cheese, milk, salt, pepper, nutmeg, and parsley; beat until smooth.
3. Melt the butter in a large sauté pan over high heat. Dredge the pork medallions in flour and dip to cover in the batter. Sauté until golden brown on each side. Remove to a serving platter.
4. Deglaze the pan over high heat with lemon juice. Pour the pan juices over the pork and serve.

At the Cottage, we serve schnitzel with roasted potatoes and a side dish of marinated vegetables.

BIBB LETTUCE SALAD WITH CELERY VINAIGRETTE DRESSING

Pinch of white pepper
1 small clove garlic, crushed
1 teaspoon salt
½ teaspoon pepper
¼ cup sugar
1 egg yolk
3 tablespoons Grey Poupon mustard

1 stalk celery
1 cubanella pepper
1 green onion
½ cup lemon juice
1 cup Benedicta grapeseed oil
3 eggs, hard-cooked
3 heads Bibb lettuce, cleaned

1. Place all the ingredients except the lemon juice, oil, hard-cooked eggs and lettuce in a blender and purée.
2. Whisk in the lemon juice, then the oil.
3. Shell and chop the hard-cooked eggs.
4. Tear the lettuce into bite-size pieces. Drizzle dressing over and toss. Garnish with chopped egg. Divide among 6 salad plates. Refrigerate before serving.

Mint vinegar may be substituted for some of the lemon juice if desired; the result is a slightly more exotic flavor. Any high-quality salad oil is acceptable if the grapeseed oil is not available.

RASPBERRY CAKE

8 cups frozen raspberries	1½ pounds French or Vienna
1 pound butter, room temperature	bread, 1 to 2 days old
	1 quart sour cream
2 to 2¾ cups granulated sugar, to taste	2 tablespoons light brown sugar

1. Thaw the raspberries, retaining the syrup.
2. Butter the inside of a 10″ spring-form pan, at least 3″ deep. Dust generously with granulated sugar.
3. Remove the crusts from the bread. Slice about ½″ thick. Butter one side of each slice. Completely line the bottom and sides of the spring-form pan, pressing the buttered side of the bread to the pan. Generously smooth additional butter over the bread-lined mold.
4. Sprinkle about ½ cup sugar over the bread. Pour half the raspberries with juice over, and sprinkle with another ½ cup sugar. Add another layer of bread, buttered side down. Smooth more butter over, then add more sugar and the remaining raspberries, as before. Finish with a final layer of bread, butter, and sugar.
5. Place a flat plate over the cake and weight evenly with cans. Place the cake on a tray and refrigerate at least 6 hours.
6. Blend the brown sugar thoroughly into the sour cream. Reserve.
7. To serve, unmold by quickly dipping the pan in hot water. Invert on a serving platter and release the spring-form pan. Serve with sweetened sour cream.

This cake may be served with crème fraîche in place of the sweetened sour cream. A garnish of fresh or frozen whole raspberries provides a nice touch.

Dinner for Four

Zuppa Pavese

Chicken Vesuvio

or

Veal Francese

Zucchini

Cenci

Wine:

Chianti Clàssico, Melini, 1973

Ermando Garbacorta, Owner

For pasta lovers, the key word is fresh. "Preparing pasta by hand still produces the finest products," explains Ermando Gambacorta, "and I am lucky to have three dedicated women to prepare mine, who are not only skilled, but also intensely proud of their ability. This pride shows in the delicacy of their noodles. We use the old recipes and the old methods."

But Italian cooking makes use of more than pasta, and Ermando's offers a wide variety of choices. The Zucchini Parmesan is the favorite for lunch. It was hard for Ermando to pick a dinner special, he says. "Even the steaks are a treat—the equal of any in Chicago. And we use milk-fed veal from Wisconsin, the most delicate available." Gambacorta continues, "I feel that Italian cooking is the finest in the world, and that we present it with the love it deserves."

Carrying this emphasis on tradition into his restaurant's decor, Gambacorta uses red, green, and white in his menus and table coverings. The large fountain in the entryway looks as if it is in a Mediterranean villa; the aromas drifting through the dining room complete the illusion.

483 Lake Cook Road
Deerfield

ZUPPA PAVESE
Chicken Soup with Poached Eggs

6 cups CHICKEN STOCK
3 tablespoons butter
4 slices Italian bread

¼ cup freshly grated
   Parmesan Cheese
4 eggs, poached

1. Place the stock in a large, heavy pot. Bring to a boil and reduce heat to a simmer.
2. Melt the butter in a frying pan and cook the bread slices on both sides until lightly browned. Remove from the pan.
3. Sprinkle the cheese over the bread. Arrange 1 slice of bread in each of 4 bowls. Place 1 egg on each of the bread slices. Gently ladle the hot Chicken Stock around the bread. Serve hot.

CHICKEN STOCK

5 pounds chicken parts
2 medium-size onions,
   quartered
4 carrots, sliced
4 stalks celery, sliced

2 turnips, sliced
3 sprigs parsley
2 teaspoons salt
½ teaspoon pepper

1. Place the chicken parts in a 6-quart pot. Add water to cover. Bring to a boil; skim off any foam that rises to the surface.
2. Add the remaining ingredients. Reduce heat, cover, and simmer for 2 hours.
3. Strain through 2 layers of cheesecloth. Refrigerate for several hours; remove the solidified fat from the top before using.

CHICKEN VESUVIO

1 (2 to 2¾-pound) broiler- fryer chicken	1 teaspoon oregano
½ cup vegetable oil	3 tablespoons minced parsley
4 white potatoes	½ teaspoon black pepper
5 cloves garlic, finely chopped	3 ounces sauterne
4 tablespoons butter	1 cup Beef Stock (see index)

1. Preheat oven to 400°. Quarter the chicken. Wash and pat dry with paper toweling.
2. Heat the oil in a large skillet over medium heat. Add the chicken and brown completely.
3. Peel and cut each potato into 6 long wedges. Add to the chicken pan and cook until brown and tender.
4. Spread the garlic over the chicken and potatoes, cooking until golden.
5. Drain the oil, add the butter, and stir until incorporated into the drippings. Sprinkle the oregano, parsley, and pepper over.
6. Add the sauterne and beef stock. Cook over medium heat for 2 minutes.
7. Place the chicken, potatoes, and gravy in an uncovered baking dish and bake in preheated oven for 8 minutes. Serve hot.

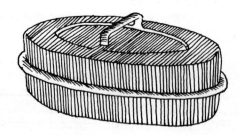

VEAL FRANCESE

2½ pounds boneless veal, steak or top round	4 eggs, beaten
2 lemons	¼ cup sauterne
¼ cup vegetable oil	1 cup Beef Stock (see index)
4 tablespoons butter, melted	Salt
Flour for dredging	Pepper

1. Slice the veal ¼″ thick. Flatten the pieces with the side of a heavy knife.
2. Slice 1 lemon in half and reserve one half. slice the remaining 1½ lemons into thin circles and reserve.
3. Heat one-third of the oil and one-third of the butter in a large sauté pan. Dredge the veal in flour to cover completely, shaking off any excess. Dip one-third of the veal in the beaten egg and sauté until golden brown, squeezing a little of the juice of the lemon half over while cooking. Remove from the pan and keep warm. Repeat for the remaining veal.
4. Add the sauterne to the veal pan and deglaze over high heat. Add the beef stock and salt and pepper to taste. Bring to a boil, reduce heat, and simmer 5 minutes.
5. Add the sliced lemon and continue to simmer for 2 to 3 minutes.
6. Return the veal to the pan to warm. Remove the veal and lemon slices with a slotted spoon; arrange alternately on a large serving platter. Taste the sauce for seasoning and adjust if necessary. Spoon the sauce over the veal and lemon. Serve.

Be careful when seasoning veal—remember that its flavor is delicate and easily overpowered.

ZUCCHINI

3 tablespoons olive oil	¾ teaspoon salt
4 stalks celery, chopped	¼ teaspoon pepper
1 small onion, chopped	1 cup bread crumbs
2 cloves garlic, minced	½ cup grated Romano cheese
1½ pounds zucchini, chopped	

1. Heat the oil in a heavy, ovenproof saucepan. Sauté the celery, onion, and garlic until tender.
2. Mix in the zucchini, salt, and pepper. Reduce heat, cover, and simmer 10 minutes.
3. Preheat oven to 375°.
4. Sprinkle the vegetables with bread crumbs and cheese and bake uncovered until the cheese has melted.

CENCI
"Rags"

3 cups all-purpose flour
¼ teaspoon salt
4 tablespoons margarine, softened
1 whole egg
1 egg yolk

¼ cup sugar
1 teaspoon vanilla extract
1 cup white wine, plus more as needed
Vegetable oil for deep-frying
Powdered sugar

1. Combine the flour and salt in a large bowl. Cut in the margarine. Lightly beat the egg, egg yolk, sugar, and vanilla extract; mix into the flour with a wooden spoon.
2. Add 1 cup wine and mix until smooth, adding more wine as needed to get the dough to form a ball. The dough should be fairly stiff.
3. Roll out to ⅛" to ¼" thickness. Cut into wide, short strips.
4. Heat enough oil to deep-fry in a large frying pan. Add the dough strips, a few at a time, and fry until golden brown. Drain on paper toweling.
5. Allow to cool and sprinkle with powdered sugar.

Store Cenci in an airtight container until ready to serve.

Le Francais

Dinner for Six

Coquilles St. Jacques, Petits Légumes

Soupe des Moules au Basilic

Pigeonneaux à Sauce l'Ail

Gâteau au Chocolat

Wine:

With the Coquilles and Soupe—Meursault, 1978

With the Pigeonneaux—Gevrey-Chambertin, 1976

Jean Banchet, Owner and Chef

LE FRANÇAIS

Jean Banchet, owner and chef of Le Français, has been called the finest chef in the land. His restaurant in Wheeling has received similar accolades, as well as countless awards and other honors. Only the freshest and foremost-quality foodstuffs are accepted into this establishment, and these from sources all over the world. From France, for example, fresh bass, truffles, and goose liver are flown in regularly. Here the most delicate of sauces and the richest of pastries are prepared in a vast kitchen hung with gleaming copper stock pots and saucepans.

Tuxedoed waiters and crimson velvet appointments set the tone in the dining room. The extensive menu changes daily and seasonally; offerings include hors d'oeuvres such as wild duck pâté and oysters in puff pastry with wine sauce and caviar, and entrées from roast breast of pheasant with morel sauce to stuffed sea bass with crabmeat.

Monsieur Banchet began his apprenticeship at age fourteen. His career since then has been studded with some of the most illustrious names in modern culinary history: Paul Bocuse's L'Auberge, the Hôtel de Paris in Monte Carlo, and the renowned Troisgros brothers are three of the best-known in this country. He followed the footsteps of many an earlier star of French cuisine when he crossed the Channel to work in London, where he met and married his charming wife, Doris. There was a short stint at the Lake Geneva (Wisconsin) Playboy Club; then he was on to Wheeling, where he opened Le Français, and American culinary history was made.

269 South Milwaukee Avenue
Wheeling

COQUILLES ST. JACQUES, PETITS LEGUMES

1½ cups milk	¾ cup thinly sliced mushrooms
Salt	
Pepper	¾ cup julienned celery
1 pound scallops	¾ cup julienned carrot
6 tablespoons butter	4½ cups sliced fresh spinach
1¼ cups clam juice	3 ounces whipping cream
1 cup Chablis	1½ tablespoons lemon juice
⅓ cup minced shallots	

1. Heat the milk to a boil. Season with salt and pepper and remove from heat.
2. Add the scallops and let stand 4 to 5 minutes or until cooked.
3. Divide the butter in half; set one half to soften at room temperature.
4. Combine the clam juice, wine, and shallots in a separate saucepan over high heat. Boil rapidly until the volume is reduced to about 1¼ cups. Reserve.
5. Separately, simmer the mushrooms, celery, and carrots in salted water for 3 minutes; drain and set the vegetables aside. In the same pan, melt the unsoftened 3 tablespoons butter and sauté the spinach just until limp. Season with salt and pepper.
6. Divide the spinach among 6 shallow baking dishes. Remove the scallops from the milk and divide over the spinach. Top with the vegetables. Keep warm in a very low oven.
7. Add the whipping cream to the clam juice/wine reduction. Boil rapidly until the mixture thickens enough to coat the back of a spoon. Whisk in the softened butter, 1 teaspoon at a time. Remove from heat. Add the lemon juice. Taste for seasonings and adjust if necessary.
8. Spoon the sauce over the scallops. Serve at once.

SOUPE DE MOULES AU BASILIC

1½ quarts fresh mussels	Pepper
5 shallots, chopped	2 cups FISH STOCK
¼ bunch parsley	1 tablespoon chopped basil
1 stalk celery, chopped	2 cups whipping cream
1 cup dry white wine	1 egg yolk, lightly beaten
Salt	¼ pound butter

1. Wash and scrape the mussels well. Place in a kettle with ½ cup water, the shallots, parsley, celery, wine, and a little salt and pepper. Bring to a boil, cover, and simmer about 6 minutes or until the shells open. Discard any that do not open.
2. Remove the mussels with a slotted spoon and reserve. Strain the liquid through a fine sieve or cheesecloth, to remove the herbs and any sand, and return to the kettle.
3. Add the Fish Stock, half the basil, and 1½ cups whipping cream. Boil, stirring, for 2 to 3 minutes. Season to taste.
4. Just before serving, mix the rest of the cream with the egg yolk and butter and add to the stock. Heat, but do not boil.
5. Remove the mussels from their shells, discarding the shells. Chop the mussels coarsely.
6. Ladle the stock into soup bowls or bouillon cups. Divide the mussels among the servings and garnish with the remaining chopped basil. Serve very hot.

FISH STOCK

1 onion	1 bay leaf
1 whole clove	1 carrot
1 pound fish trimings	1 stalk celery, sliced
(head, tail, and bones)	1 teaspoon salt
1½ quarts cold water	4 white peppercorns

Cut a slit in the onion and insert the whole clove. Place all ingredients in a stock pot over medium-low heat and bring slowly to a boil. Skim any foam that accumulates on the surface. Simmer 45 minutes. Strain through a fine sieve before using.

Leftover fish stock should be stored in 1 and 2-cup containers for convenience. It may be frozen.

PIGEONNEAUX A SAUCE L'AIL

Have your butcher bone the squab without cutting them open, or do it yourself by the directions following this recipe.

36	unpeeled garlic cloves	½	cup Chicken Stock (see index)
6	(14-ounce) squab, cleaned and boned, livers reserved	3	tablespoons brandy
	Salt	24	medium-size mushrooms, trimmed
	Freshly ground black pepper		CHICKEN QUENELLES (see next page)
7	tablespoons unsalted butter		
½	cup Chablis		

1. Preheat oven to 450°. Poach the garlic in boiling water for 4 minutes; drain.
2. Season the squab lightly with salt and pepper. Melt 4 tablespoons butter in a large ovenproof skillet over medium-high heat. Add the squab and sauté until browned on all sides. Add 12 garlic cloves and brown quickly.
3. Transfer to preheated oven and roast, basting occasionally, until the squab are done—20 to 25 minutes. Transfer the squab and garlic to a serving platter and keep warm.
4. Deglaze the skillet with the wine. Peel 12 of the garlic cloves; crush with the flat of a knife and add to the skillet. Set aside.
5. Melt 1 tablespoon butter in a small skillet over medium-high heat. Add the reserved squab livers and sauté until evenly browned but still pink inside.
6. Transfer to a blender or food processor and purée to a paste. Add a bit of the wine mixture and blend well. Stir the livers back into the remaining wine mixture.
7. Add the chicken stock and brandy, place the pan over low heat, and simmer until the sauce is heated through.
8. Melt the remaining 2 tablespoons butter in a large skillet over medium heat. Add the mushrooms and sauté until golden. Pour the liver sauce over the squab. Garnish the platter with the sautéed mushrooms, remaining garlic cloves, and Chicken Quenelles. Serve immediately.

Note: To bone squab:
1. Flash-freeze the squab until some ice crystals have formed.
2. Clean out the cavity. Rinse the bird under cool water and pat dry with paper towels.
3. Trim the wings at the joint, discarding the tips. Stand the bird upright. Using a sharp knife, cut through the wings where they join the body.
4. Loosen the meat from the breast bones by inserting fingers between the meat and skeleton along the keel bone and pushing against the bone, toward the bottom. (You may want to scrape with the knife from time to time instead of using just your fingers, in order to get all the meat.) Do not be concerned if small bits of meat come off the skin-bound mass; any small pieces may be returned to the cavity after boning.
5. Turn the bird over onto its breast and carefully loosen the meat from the back by pushing with fingers or scraping with a knife. Gradually turn the skin inside-out as you work.
6. Cut the thigh bones at the joints with scissors and complete the boning, reserving the skeleton for stock.
7. Turn the boned bird right-side-out again, feeling for any overlooked small bones.

This method of boning is called 'glove boning'.

CHICKEN QUENELLES

Makes about 6 dozen small quenelles.

1 pound boned and skinned
   chicken breast
1 teaspoon salt
½ teaspoon freshly ground
   pepper
¼ teaspoon freshly grated
   nutmeg

2 egg whites, lightly beaten
2 cups whipping cream
   Salted water or chicken
   stock for poaching

1. Grind the chicken finely in a processor or meat grinder. Add the salt, pepper, and nutmeg and blend well.
2. Gradually add the egg whites, mixing vigorously after each addition.
3. Gradually add the cream and mix until firm enough to hold its shape. (If mixing by hand: when adding the cream, set the bowl into a larger bowl filled with cracked ice. Beat in the cream by the tablespoon.)
4. Generously butter a large skillet. Dip 2 teaspoons into boiling water. Heap 1 spoon with the chicken paste and round off with the other. Dip the second spoon into hot water again, slip it under the paste oval, and slide the quenelle into the buttered skillet. Repeat until the quenelles line the skillet in a single layer without crowding.
5. Slowly add enough hot salted water or stock to the skillet to float the quenelles. Bring the liquid to a simmer over low heat and poach the quenelles until firm, about 5 to 10 minutes. Do not allow the liquid to come to a boil.
6. Remove the quenelles with a slotted spoon and drain well on paper towels. Repeat the shaping and cooking procedures for the remaining batter.

GÂTEAU AU CHOCOLAT

14 ounces Ghirardelli semisweet baking chocolate	10 eggs, separated
¼ pound plus 6 tablespoons unsalted butter	1 tablespoon Grand Marnier
1½ cups granulated sugar	1 teaspoon vanilla extract
	CRÈME ANGLAISE
	Confectioners' sugar

1. Preheat oven to 250°.
2. Break the chocolate into chunks and place with the butter in the top of a double boiler. Melt over simmering water, stirring occasionally.
3. Stir 1¼ cups sugar into the melted chocolate and continue heating until the sugar is almost dissolved.
4. Beat the egg yolks in a separate bowl. Beat some of the hot chocolate mixture into the yolks, then beat the yolk mixture into the remaining chocolate. Cook over simmering water, stirring constantly, until slightly thickened. Remove from heat and allow to cool.
5. Stir in the Grand Marnier and vanilla extract.
6. Beat the egg whites until they stand in soft peaks when the beater or whisk is removed. Continue beating, gradually adding the remaining ¼ cup sugar, until the whites stand upright in stiff peaks.
7. Spoon one-third of the chocolate mixture over the beaten egg whites and fold together carefully. Add remaining chocolate and continue to fold just until incorporated. Spoon into a buttered and floured 12″ springform pan.
8. Bake in preheated oven for 3 hours. Let cool to room temperature, then cover and refrigerate at least 3 hours.
9. Transfer the cake to a serving platter and dust with confectioners' sugar. Place the cooled Crème Anglaise in a serving bowl. Cut the cake in small wedges; serve with a few spoonfuls of Crème Anglaise.

LE FRANÇAIS

CRÈME ANGLAISE

2½ cups milk
8 egg yolks, beaten

1¼ cups granulated sugar
2 vanilla beans

1. Heat the milk to a boil in a medium saucepan.
2. In a separate bowl, whisk the egg yolks and granulated sugar until ribbons form when dropped from the whisk. Whisk a little of the hot milk into the mixture, then whisk the yolks into the remaining milk.
3. Add the vanilla beans and stir over low heat until the custard coats the back of a spoon. Do not allow to boil.
4. Immediately spoon the Crème Anglaise into a bowl and set in a pan of ice water to cool. Remove the vanilla beans.

FROGGY'S

Dinner for Four

Gâteau de Carrottes aux Crevettes de Mattane

Sliced Calves' Liver with Raspberries and Onions

Purée of Turnips

Petits Pots de Crème au Café

Wine:

Pouilly-Fuissé

Greg Mason, Owner

Thierry Lefeuvre, Chef

If you subscribe to the wisdom of the old axiom that a restaurant is no better than its kitchen, you won't be at all surprised at the success of Froggy's: Thierry Lefeuvre, its young Brêton chef, is a master at his craft. Because his creations are a treat for the eye as well as the palate, the restaurant, as an aid to the undecided diner, displays the specials of the day in the window facing the entrance. From the unique beginning until the last melting morsel of dessert, dinner or lunch at Froggy's is an adventure in light, classical French food at its best.

A first course may consist of a lobster pâté, a layered tour de force in shades of pink, with spinach mousse tucked in between the layers, and decorated with a lobster claw. Or perhaps a pâté of duck, or a molded venison pâté in puff pastry with a Madeira sauce. Next on the menu you may find veal slices napped with an orange and wine sauce, or fresh *fruits de mer* rushed from the source—perhaps Boston sole served with mussels and saffron, or bay scallops on a bed of sweet onions with a peppercorn sauce. Sweetbreads are served in a pastry shell with mushrooms and a ginger sauce; French sausage is cooked with red wine and shallots. Dessert may vary from a chilled raspberry soufflé garnished with sauce and fresh red raspberries, or a chocolate mousse cake surrounded by white chocolate sauce, to sliced pears sautéed in wine sauce, covered with pastry and ice cream.

A further indication of the serious attention given to cooking is that the kitchens are virtually as large as the dining area. Here, huge walk-in refrigerators bursting with fresh meats, fruits, and vegetables and vast cauldrons of slowly simmering stocks await the attentions of the large staff.

As Chef Lefeuvre observes in an amplification of the restaurant's philosophy, "We are dedicated to producing superb French food. Our customer is assured that he will receive the finest that the marketplace has to offer in an atmosphere, and at a price, that will encourage and allow him to dine here often."

306 Green Bay Road
Highwood

GÂTEAU DE CARROTTES AUX CREVETTES DE MATTANE
Carrot Mousse Cake, Garnished with Shrimp

½ pound Mattane shrimp
Salt
1 pound carrots, scrubbed
½ onion, thinly sliced
1 cup white wine
¼ pound butter
1 shallot, chopped

Pepper to taste
Nutmeg
2 eggs
½ cup whipping cream
2 ounces Swiss cheese, grated
1 teaspoon cornstarch

1. Boil the shrimp for 3 to 4 minutes, or until barely cooked, in 2 cups water and 1½ teaspoons salt. Remove the shrimp with a slotted spoon. Remove the shrimp from the shells and reserve; return the shells to the pot. Chop ½ carrot and add to the pot, along with the sliced onion and wine. Return to a boil, reduce heat, and simmer 20 minutes. Strain and reserve.
2. Cut the remaining carrots into 1" slices. Melt the butter in a heavy pan; add the chopped shallot and sauté until soft. Add the carrots, 2 cups strained shrimp stock, and salt, pepper, and nutmeg to taste. Return to a boil, reduce heat, and simmer until the carrots are tender and the stock is a thick reduction. Remove from heat and let cool to room temperature.
3. Combine the cooked vegetables with the eggs, cream, Swiss cheese, and cornstarch. Purée in 2 batches in a blender or food processor. (Taste and adjust seasonings if necessary.)
4. Preheat oven to 350°.
5. Combine the vegetable mixture with half the cooked shrimp. Divide the mixture among 6 buttered custard cups and place in a deep baking pan. Add hot water to a depth of 1 inch.
6. Bake in preheated oven for 15 minutes or until a knife inserted in the middle of one cake comes out perfectly clean.
7. Allow to cool. Run a knife around the edges of the cups and invert onto individual dishes. Garnish with the remaining cooked shrimp and serve.

This recipe makes six servings; leftovers may be enjoyed hot or cold the next day.

FROGGY'S FRENCH CAFE

SLICED CALVES' LIVER WITH RASPBERRIES AND ONIONS

3 small Spanish onions, thinly sliced in rings
2 tablespoons butter
1 pint raspberries
Salt and pepper to taste

1 pound calves' liver, thinly sliced
½ cup raspberry vinegar
½ cup Veal Stock (see index)

1. In a large skillet, sauté the onion rings in 1 tablespoon butter until soft and golden brown. Set aside one-third of the onions; stir three-fourths of the raspberries into the remainder. Cook no more than 30 seconds so as not to break down the berries. Season to taste with salt and pepper. Remove to a hot serving platter; keep warm.
2. Add the remaining butter to the skillet over medium-high heat. Add the liver slices, a few at a time, and cook until browned, about 30 seconds per side. Arrange over the onion/raspberry mixture on the serving platter.
3. Stir the vinegar into the pan juices to deglaze. Cook over high heat for 1 minute. Add the veal stock and stir well. Reduce heat and simmer until the mixture is reduced to half its original volume. Taste and adjust seasonings.
4. Place the reserved sautéed onion and the reserved raspberries over the liver slices and spoon the pan sauce over.

Serve with fresh vegetables.

PURÉE OF TURNIPS

1 to 1¼ pounds turnips, cut into
        1" chunks
    1 potato, peeled, cut into
        ½" chunks

    ½ teaspoon salt
    ¼ teaspoon white pepper
    ½ cup whipping cream
    2 tablespoons butter

1. Place the turnips and potato in a saucepan. Cover with water, sprinkle with the salt, and simmer until the vegetables are tender, about 25 minutes.
2. Drain the vegetables and mash well. Return to the saucepan. Add the pepper, cream, and butter. Stir to combine and heat gently until the butter melts. Serve hot.

PETITS POTS DE CRÈME AU CAFÉ
Pots of Coffee Cream

    4 eggs
    3 tablespoons sugar
    3 tablespoons strong-brewed
        coffee

    1 tablespoon extra-fine
        instant coffee
    1 tablespoon Kahlua
    2 cups milk

1. Preheat oven to 275°.
2. Place the eggs, sugar, and coffees in a large mixing bowl. Mix well. Add the Kahlua and milk.
3. Fill 4 custard cups with the mixture. Place in a deep baking pan filled with 1" hot water. Bake in preheated oven for 45 minutes or until a knife inserted in the center comes out clean.

Serve warm or cold.

Hans' Bavarian Lodge

Dinner for Four

Rollmops

Austrian Salad

Almond Schnitzel

Cheese Noodles with Paprika

Blitz Torte

Rüdesheimer Coffee

Wine:

Moselblümchen

Jane Berghoff, Owner
Shay Roman, Chef

HANS' BAVARIAN LODGE

Platters of bratwursts, pitchers of beer, bowls of sauerkraut, toe-tapping polka rhythms, and hundreds of revelers fill the vast blue-and-white-striped tent outside of Hans' Bavarian Lodge every fall for an authentic Oktoberfest celebration. The tent accommodates twenty-five hundred guests. The Oktoberfest consists of continuous entertainment and excellent German Food and drink. *Gemütlichkeit* is the German word for friendliness, hospitality, and warmth, and is usually associated with food. Lovers of gemütlichkeit as well as of plain good fun come from all over the area to join in the festivities, just as those who appreciate excellent German food come here all year long.

The outside of the building is decorated by the coats of arms of many houses of ancient Germany. There is no doubt that when you cross the doorway you are transported to Europe. The Lodge is divided into several cozy rooms, with a fireplace, beamed ceiling, stained-glass windows, and walls adorned with Germanic scenes. Even the names of various German cities find their way into the menu as names of specialties. We find Heidelburg Roast Beef, as well as Hamburg Chopped Beef, on the menu.

The specialty of the house is schnitzel; one may be entertained by the fact that there is a different schnitzel entrée for each day of the week. Wiener schnitzel, rostbraten, kassler rippochen, and sauerbraten star on a menu rich with the tastes of the Rhineland. German Chocolate Cake, Black Forest Cake, kuchens and strudels, cheesecakes and bavarians, pies and tortes; the rewards at the end of the meal are as satisfying as those in the beginning.

931 North Milwaukee Avenue
Wheeling

ROLLMOPS

4 filets Matjes herring	16 capers
1 tablespoon Dusseldorf mustard	1 cup white wine
1 kosher dill pickle, cut into julienne strips	½ cup white vinegar
1½ Bermuda onions, shaved into thin onion rings	1 tablespoon whole mixed pickling spices

1. Lay the herring filets flat. Spread a thin layer of mustard over each filet.
2. Arrange 2 to 3 strips of pickle, 2 to 3 onion rings, and 3 to 4 capers on each filet. Roll up jelly-roll fashion and secure with toothpicks if necessary.
3. Combine the white wine, vinegar, pickling spices, and remaining onion. Place rollmops into the marinade. Allow to marinate 3 to 4 days before serving.

AUSTRIAN SALAD

1 head escarole	White vinegar
¼ pound bacon	Freshy ground black pepper
2 Idaho potatoes	Salt

1. Bake the potatoes at 350° for 1 hour or until done. While still warm, remove the skins. Dice the potatoes in about ½" cubes.
2. Clean and chop the escarole. Place in ice water for about 20 minutes. Drain and pat dry. Place in a large salad bowl.
3. Fry the bacon. Drain and crumble, reserving ¼ cup drippings.
4. Add the hot drippings, hot potatoes, and vinegar to taste to the escarole. Sprinkle the crumbled bacon over. Season to taste with freshly ground pepper and salt. Toss and serve immediately.

ALMOND SCHNITZEL

2 eggs, beaten
¾ cup sour cream
4 veal cutlets, pounded thin
¾ cup crushed almonds
½ cup bread crumbs
¼ teaspoon salt

⅛ teaspoon white pepper
2 tablespoons butter
2 tablespoons margarine
¼ cup whipping cream
½ cup toasted almonds

1. Mix the eggs with ½ cup sour cream and set aside.
2. Combine the crushed almonds, bread crumbs, salt, and pepper; set aside.
3. In a heavy saucepan, melt the butter and margarine. Dip the cutlets into the egg/sour cream mixture and then into the almond/bread crumb mixture. Quickly sauté the schnitzels over high heat until golden brown on each side. Remove from heat and pat dry.
4. Combine the remaining sour cream and the whipping cream.
5. Arrange the schnitzels on a heated serving platter. Pour the sour cream sauce over and sprinkle with the toasted almonds.

HANS' BAVARIAN LODGE

CHEESE NOODLES WITH PAPRIKA

1 cup sour cream
2 tablespoons whipping cream
2 tablespoons butter
2 tablespoons grated
   Parmesan cheese
½ pound medium egg noodles,
   cooked and drained

Salt and pepper to taste
½ pound extra-sharp cheddar
   cheese, grated
Paprika

1. Preheat oven to 350°.
2. In a small, heavy saucepan, melt the sour cream with the whipping cream, butter, and Parmesan cheese.
3. Fold the cooked noodles into the sour cream mixture. Sprinkle with salt and pepper to taste. Add half the grated cheddar cheese. Fold the mixture once again.
4. Place into a buttered 9″ by 9″ by 2″ baking pan. Top with the remaining grated cheddar cheese. Sprinkle lightly with paprika. Bake in preheated oven until bubbly, about 25 minutes.

BLITZ TORTE

3 egg whites, room temperature
2¼ cups plus 1½ tablespoons sugar
¾ cup unsalted butter
3¼ cups sifted cake flour
3½ teaspoons baking powder
⅛ teaspoon salt
1 cup less 1 tablespoon milk
1½ teaspoons vanilla extract
3 whole eggs, lightly beaten
⅓ cup slivered almonds
PINEAPPLE FILLING

1. Preheat oven to 350°.
2. Beat the egg whites until foamy and soft peaks form. Gradually add ¾ cup sugar, ¼ cup at a time. Beat until the egg whites are stiff and all the sugar has been incorporated; set aside.
3. Cream the butter and the remaining sugar until light.
4. Combine the cake flour, baking powder, and salt. Mix into the butter mixture until combined.
5. Combine the milk and vanilla. Beat into the batter for 2 minutes. Add the beaten whole eggs and beat for 1 minute.
6. Pour the mixture into a greased 9″ spring-form pan. Spread the reserved meringue over and sprinkle with slivered almonds. Bake in preheated oven about 55 minutes (35 minutes if using a convection oven), or until a cake tester inserted in the center comes out clean.
7. Allow to cool 10 minutes. Remove from the spring-form pan and let cool completely. Slice into 3 layers. Fill layers with Pineapple Filling.

Another way to test the cake's doneness is to press on the center. It should rebound at once to its original shape if done.

PINEAPPLE FILLING

6 tablespoons sugar
1½ tablespoons flour
Dash of salt
3 egg yolks, beaten
1 cup milk
1½ tablespoons unsalted butter
1½ cups crushed pineapple, drained

1. Combine the sugar, flour, and salt in the top of a double boiler. Stir in the beaten egg yolks and milk.
2. Stir over boiling water until the mixture thickens. Remove from heat and mix in the butter and crushed pineapple. Continue stirring until the butter has melted. Allow to cool before using.

RÜDESHEIMER COFFEE

½ cup whipping cream, chilled
1 teaspoon vanilla extract
8 cubes sugar
8 ounces Asbach brandy

Freshly brewed coffee
¼ cup shaved semisweet chocolate

1. Whip the cream with the vanilla; reserve.
2. Warm 4 cups or mugs with hot water; pour the water off. Place 2 to 3 cubes of sugar in each cup. Add 1½ to 2 ounces Asbach brandy per cup. If desired, flame the brandy, stir, and allow to burn for 1 minute.
3. Fill the cups with good hot coffee to within an inch of the top and stir well. Cover with a layer of whipped cream and sprinkle with shaved chocolate.

Asbach Uralt is an excellent German brandy.

A hint for shaving chocolate: have the chocolate at room temperature and shave with a potato peeler, working over waxed paper. Always shave downwards.

Kingston Harbour Yacht Club

Dinner for Six

Bay Scallops

Bookbinder Soup

Salad served with Croissants

Sea Bass in Pastry Crust

Ratatouille

Frozen Lemon Soufflé

Wine:

With the Scallops—Sancerre, 1979
With the Soup—Findlater's Dry Fly Medium Sherry
With the Bass—Mâcon Blanc, Jadot
With the Soufflé—Domaine Chandon Brut

Weiland Ludwig, Owner and Chef

KINGSTON HARBOUR YACHT CLUB

Lush tropical foliage and rushing waterfalls reminiscent of a Jamaican garden provide the backdrop for diners at the Kingston Harbour Yacht Club. The vaulted ceilings add to the drama of the building, and thirteen spacious levels, including a dancing area, multiply the romantic feeling of this restaurant. It is decorated with rattan furniture and orange tones, reflecting a Caribbean island atmosphere. "We wanted to bring the relaxing, romantic spirit of the tropics into our restaurant," states one of the three partners. "But we knew that atmosphere is only one part of a dining experience. The food must warrant the setting.

"In keeping with this recognition, we use only the freshest of fish in our dishes. Dover sole is flown in from France, and other seafood is rushed from both coasts. Our menu, which includes soft-shell crabs, frogs' legs, and lobster, is dependent on the fresh fish available each season. The exception is Sea Bass en Croûte—it is such a favorite that we try to have it on our menu as often as possible."

The man responsible for carrying out the menu, Chef Weiland Ludwig, supervises his workers in a custom-designed, gleaming, stainless-steel and tile kitchen. Included in his twelve-person staff is a special bread chef, an increasingly rare breed in today's establishments.

700 North River Road
Mount Prospect

BAY SCALLOPS

2 tablespoons butter
1 medium-size onion,
  chopped
2 cloves garlic, minced
1 cup sliced mushrooms
1¼ pounds bay scallops

Salt and pepper to taste
¼ cup white wine
2 tablespoons all-purpose
  flour
Parsley sprigs for garnish

1. Heat the butter in a skillet over medium-low heat. Sauté the onions, garlic, and mushrooms until soft.
2. Add the bay scallops and sprinkle with salt and pepper. Sauté until the scallops are opaque.
3. Mix in the white wine and sprinkle with the flour. Continue cooking until the flour is absorbed and the mixture thickens slightly.
4. Serve in scallop-shell dishes, garnished with parsley sprigs.

Be careful in cooking scallops, as they tend to get rubbery if overcooked.

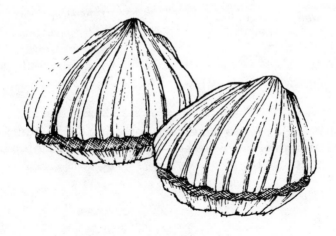

BOOKBINDER SOUP

4 tablespoons butter	1⅓ cups FISH STOCK
1 cup diced onions	1⅓ cups demi-glace
1 cup diced green peppers	1⅓ cups tomato sauce
1 cup diced celery	1 cup sherry
1 cup diced red snapper or grouper filet	

1. Melt the butter in a 3-quart pot over medium heat. Sauté the onion, green pepper, and celery until soft. Add the snapper and sauté for 5 minutes.
2. Mix in the Fish Stock, demi-glace, and tomato sauce and bring to a boil. Reduce heat to simmer and mix in the sherry. Simmer 5 minutes. Serve hot in soup bowls.

FISH STOCK

1 pound fish, including bones, heads and skins	1 bay leaf
1 onion, sliced	¼ teaspoon thyme
1 carrot, sliced	4 peppercorns
1 stalk celery, sliced	½ cup dry white wine
	5 cups water

Combine all ingredients in a large stock pot. Bring the mixture to a boil, reduce heat, and simmer uncovered for 45 minutes. Strain through a double thickness of cheesecloth.

Makes 1 quart stock.

SALAD SERVED WITH CROISSANTS

1 onion, chopped
½ cup chopped celery
1 clove garlic, minced
½ cup salad oil
½ cup vinegar
½ cup water
   Salt and pepper to taste
1 tablespoon lemon juice

1 pound mushrooms, sliced
1 large head Boston lettuce, cleaned
6 tomatoes, sliced
   DRESSING
3 tablespoons chopped basil
6 fresh, warm CROISSANTS (see next page)

1. Combine the first 8 ingredients in a bowl. Whisk well. Add the sliced mushrooms and stir to coat. Cover and marinate 6 hours.
2. Arrange the lettuce leaves and sliced tomatoes on 6 chilled salad plates. Drizzle with Dressing and chopped basil to taste.
3. Stir the mushrooms. Remove from the marinade with a slotted spoon and distribute over the salads. Serve with warm Croissants.

DRESSING

½ cup oil
2 tablespoons vinegar
2 tablespoons freshly squeezed lemon juice

½ teaspoon salt
¼ teaspoon dry mustard

Place all ingredients in a bowl. Beat with a whisk or rotary beater until thoroughly combined. Place in a covered container and refrigerate until ready to use. Shake before using.

Olive oil, perhaps combined with a lighter salad oil, works well for this recipe.

CROISSANTS

1 tablespoon active dry yeast	½ teaspoon salt
1 tablespoon sugar	1 teaspoon salad oil
2 cups all-purpose flour, plus more for dusting	¼ pound unsalted butter, room temperature
¾ cup milk, scalded and cooled to room temperature	

1. Place ¼ cup water at 105° to 115° (warm, not hot, to touch) in a measuring cup. Stir in the yeast to dissolve. Sprinkle 1 teaspoon sugar over the mixture and stir lightly to dissolve. Set aside 10 to 15 minutes to proof.
2. Measure the 2 cups flour into a mixing bowl. Make a well in the center and add the remaining sugar, milk, salt, salad oil, and yeast mixture. Mix in the flour quickly with your fingertips. Turn out onto a lightly floured board.
3. If the dough is not smooth, knead gently 1 to 2 minutes. Form into a ball and place in a greased bowl. Turn so that the top is greased. Cover with a damp cloth and allow to rise in a warm place until almost doubled in bulk, about 2 hours.
4. Punch the dough back down. Turn out onto a lightly floured board and roll into an approximately 14″ by 7″ or 8″ rectangle.
5. Cut the butter into pats ½″ thick. Arrange the pats to cover two-thirds of the dough rectangle. Fold the unbuttered end of the rectangle over the middle third of the dough, and fold the exposed (buttered) third over all. Each of the three layers should be as accurate as possible; if necessary, pull on the corners of the dough to keep them square and even.
6. Roll the dough again, this time to a rectangle about 12″ to 14″ by 6″, and fold in thirds as before. Dust lightly with flour, cover well with plastic wrap, and refrigerate 1 hour. Repeat this process (rolling out, folding in thirds, and refrigerating) two more times.
7. Cut the dough in half. Roll each half separately on a lightly floured board into a rectangle about 8″ wide and ⅛″ thick. Cut into 4″ squares; cut these diagonally into triangles. Roll up each triangle, starting from the long side. Seal the pointed ends with a little water.
8. Set 2″ apart on an ungreased baking sheet, curling the ends into a crescent shape if desired. Cover with a cloth and set to rise 1 hour in a warm, draft-free place.
9. Preheat oven to 375°. Bake the croissants about 25 minutes, or until golden and crisp.

This recipe makes about 2½ dozen. Croissants may be kept 2 to 3 days in an air-tight container, or may be frozen before or after baking.

SEA BASS IN PASTRY CRUST

1 *onion, chopped*	1½ *pounds puff pastry*
1 *tablespoon butter*	6 *(4 to 6-ounce) portions*
3 *cloves garlic, minced*	*black or striped sea bass filets*
¾ *pound leaf spinach, chopped*	2 *eggs, lightly beaten*
Salt and pepper to taste	1 *lemon, sliced*
Nutmeg to taste	*SEAFOOD MOUSSE*
2 *tablespoons Pernod*	

1. Sauté the onion in the butter until soft. Add the garlic, spinach, salt, pepper, and nutmeg; stir and allow to come back up to heat. Add the Pernod and mix well. Remove from heat and allow to cool.
2. Preheat oven to 375°.
3. Roll the puff pastry to ¼" thick on a floured board. Cut out 2 pieces for each portion of fish, large enough to cover the fish with 1½" to spare all the way around.
4. Place each portion of fish on a piece of pastry. Divide the spinach mixture over. Top with Seafood Mousse. Cover with the remaining pieces of pastry, pressing firmly at the edges to seal.
5. Brush the pastries with the beaten egg. Trim into fish shapes, forming eyes and fins with the trimmings.
6. Line a baking sheet with parchment paper. Place the pastries on it and bake in preheated oven for 25 minutes or until golden brown. Garnish with lemon slices and serve.

SEAFOOD MOUSSE

¾ pound filets of sea trout
   or other fish
1 pint whipping cream
3 tablespoons cognac

Salt and pepper to taste
1 tablespoon lemon juice
3 eggs

Grind the fish finely in a food processor or meat grinder. Add the remaining ingredients and mix well. Refrigerate until ready to use.

RATATOUILLE

1 eggplant
1 zucchini
2 onions
2 green peppers
6 tomatoes

6 tablespoons olive oil
1 clove garlic, crushed
   Salt and pepper to taste
2 bay leaves

Wash the vegetables and cut into 1″ pieces. Heat the oil in a large skillet. Sauté the vegetables individually until tender; combine in a large bowl. Add the garlic, salt, pepper, and bay leaves and toss well. Remove the bay leaves before serving.

Ratatouille is good hot or cold, and refrigerates well.

FROZEN LEMON SOUFFLÉ

4 lemons
¾ cup sugar
6 eggs, separated

6 crystallized violets
1 cup whipping cream, whipped

1. Grate the zest of the lemons. Squeeze the juice into a bowl; add the zest, sugar, and egg yolks. Beat well.
2. Whip the egg whites until stiff peaks form. Fold the lemon mixture in well.
3. Cut 6 (2"-wide) strips of paper. Affix with tape to 6 soufflé cups to form collars extending up past the rims of the cups. Fill the cups with the lemon mixture and freeze at least 2 hours before serving.
4. Remove the soufflés to room temperature 5 minutes before serving. Garnish with crystallized violets and whipped cream.

THE KING'S WHARF

Dinner for Six

Seafood Gumbo

Salad Rossini with Mustard Dressing

Filet of Sole Oscar

Mile-High Ice Cream Pie

Wine:

Chardonnay, 1978

Daniel Christl, Restaurant Manager

KING'S WHARF

The name of this establishment is derived from the folktale of the wharf that continued to give the bounties of the world to its king. That wharf is said to have supplied its king his every desire, from opals to exotic foods. It is therefore only appropriate that the King's Wharf Restaurant should be so named. Dedicated to the preparation of fine fish and shellfish, the King's Wharf offers a seafood bar, weekday buffet lunch, and Sunday champagne brunch in addition to the dinner menu, abundant with the fruits of the sea.

The King's Wharf is situated on the first floor of Marriott's Lincolnshire luxury resort complex. As one enters the restaurant there is only a vague awareness that one is treading up a ship's ramp, but from that moment on, one is surrounded by nautical themes. Overhead are lobster traps, colorful buoys, and fishnets tastefully placed throughout the dining rooms. The many levels of the restaurant suggest the decks of a ship; one even looks out on the brooks and gardens of the beautifully manicured grounds with the sensation of being at anchor in the private harbor of some foreign nobleman.

Specialties of the house include Lobster Thermidor, schrod, salmon, and oysters flown in from either coast. Prime cuts of beef are available for meat lovers, as well as succulent poultry items. Desserts are another specialty, featuring French pastries and English trifles prepared by an in-house pastry chef.

Marriott's Lincolnshire Resort
Lincolnshire

SEAFOOD GUMBO

6 tablespoons butter
6 tablespoons all-purpose flour
½ cup diced celery
1 small red or green pepper, diced
1 medium-size onion, chopped
1 to 2 cloves garlic, minced
1½ quarts Fish Stock (see index)

3 cups canned tomatoes, chopped
6 ounces crabmeat, cleaned
½ pound small shrimp
1 teaspoon thyme
½ teaspoon cayenne powder
¼ teaspoon black pepper
1 bay leaf
1 cup sliced okra
1 tablespoon gumbo filé

1. Melt the butter in a 4-quart saucepan over medium heat. Add the flour and stir frequently until the roux becomes an even chocolate brown without burning, about 20 minutes.
2. Add the celery, pepper, and onion to the mixture. Simmer until the vegetables are tender.
3. Add the garlic and stir. Add the fish stock, tomatoes, crab, shrimp, thyme, cayenne, black pepper, bay leaf, and okra. Return to a simmer and cook until the okra is tender, about 45 minutes.
4. Mix the gumbo filé with a little water to make a paste. Turn off the heat under the soup and stir the filé in. Remove the bay leaf. Allow to sit a few minutes before serving.

One great way to enjoy this soup is to place a large spoonful of cooked rice in a bowl and ladle the gumbo around and over.

Do not boil gumbo filé—it becomes stringy.

SALAD ROSSINI WITH MUSTARD DRESSING

1 *bunch curly endive,*
washed and drained
1 *bunch watercress, washed*
and drained
1 *bunch dandelion greens,*
washed and drained

3 *papayas*
3 *stalks celery, sliced*
MUSTARD DRESSING

1. Spin or towel-dry the greens and tear into bite-size pieces. Reserve one-third of the greens; arrange the remainder on 6 chilled salad plates.
2. Slice the papayas in half. Remove the seeds and peels. Place 1 half on each salad plate.
3. Arrange the reserved greens over the papayas. Sprinkle the celery over. Drizzle each serving with Mustard Dressing.

MUSTARD DRESSING

2 *teaspoons prepared*
Dijon mustard
2 *egg yolks, well beaten*

1 *cup olive oil*
⅓ *cup lemon juice*

Combine the mustard and egg yolks in a mixing bowl. Mix in the olive oil and lemon juice, blending well.

KING'S WHARF

FILET OF SOLE OSCAR

30 medium-size asparagus
    spears
6 (6-ounce) filets of sole
    Salt and pepper
    Flour for dredging

3 eggs, lightly beaten
½ cup clarified butter
¾ pound Alaskan king
    crab meat
2 cups HOLLANDAISE SAUCE

1. Steam the asparagus spears until just tender but still very green. Refrigerate until needed.
2. Season the sole with salt and pepper. Dip in flour to coat lightly. Dip into the beaten egg to cover completely.
3. Heat about ¼ cup clarified butter in a skillet over high heat. Sauté the sole filets on each side until light golden. Remove to heated plates; keep warm.
4. Sauté the crab in a separate pan in about 2 tablespoons clarified butter to heat through.
5. Sauté the asparagus in 2 tablespoons clarified butter to heat. Place 5 asparagus spears across each sautéed piece of sole, tips all pointing in the same direction. Top each with crabmeat. Cover the crabmeat with Hollandaise sauce.
6. Place the plates under a hot broiler for a few seconds to glaze. Serve immediately.

Be sure not to brown the sauce while you have the dish under the broiler, only glaze it.

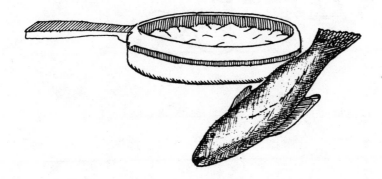

HOLLANDAISE SAUCE
for the blender

6 egg yolks
¼ cup fresh squeezed
   lemon juice

¼ teaspoon salt
¼ teaspoon cayenne pepper
1 cup clarified butter

1. Place the egg yolks, lemon juice, salt, and cayenne in a blender and blend.
2. Heat the butter over very low heat. Do not simmer or brown.
3. With the blender at low speed, add the butter gradually to the egg yolk mixture. Continue to blend for 12 to 15 seconds. The sauce should be thickened and smooth; if not, blend 5 seconds at high speed.

Makes about 2 cups.

MILE-HIGH ICE CREAM PIE

⅓ cup butter
½ cup sugar
1⅓ cups graham cracker crumbs
1 quart chocolate ice cream,
   softened
3 egg whites,
   room temperature

½ teaspoon cream of tartar
1½ cups chocolate sauce
¼ cup Grand Marnier
2 tablespoons rum

1. Melt the butter in a small saucepan over low heat. Stir in ¼ cup sugar to dissolve. Remove pan from heat.
2. Place the cracker crumbs in a mixing bowl. Add the butter/sugar mixture and mix well to blend. Pat into a 9½" pie pan.
3. Spread the ice cream into the crust. Freeze 1 hour.
4. Preheat oven to 475°.
5. Beat the egg whites with an electric mixer until soft peaks form. Sprinkle in the cream of tartar and the remaining ¼ cup sugar, one tablespoon at a time, while continuing to beat until stiff peaks form.
6. Spread the meringue over the pie and bake in preheated oven only until the meringue is lightly browned, about 2 minutes.
7. Heat the chocolate sauce in a saucepan over low heat. Stir in the Grand Marnier and rum.
8. Cut the pie into serving portions. Dress with chocolate sauce.

Dinner for Six

Sangría

Sopa de Ajo

Guacamole

Garnachas

Chiles Rellenos

Asado de Plátanos

Sopa de Arroz

Calabacitas con Crema

Flán

Wine:

With the Garnachas—Brillante

With the Asado—Los Reyes

Cesar A. Dovalina, Owner

Mrs. Olga Flores and Salvador Nova, Managers

Vicente Villa, Chef

LA MARGARITA

Soft lights and tasteful Mexican decorations highlight La Margarita restaurant. Large stained-glass windows represent the Aztec zodiac; gold tablecloths are accented by deep red napkins; white stucco walls and an open fireplace are flanked by handsome blue and white Pueblo tiles. Each table is set with a tangy green pepper sauce, crisp tortilla chips, and a plentiful dish of pickled vegetables. Piñatas hang from the walls, and carved woods combine to create a warm atmosphere further enhanced by original carved statues set in the walls.

La Margarita's owner, Cesar A. Dovalina, is from Mexico. His menu development draws on his twenty years in the restaurant business. The extensive menu includes personal favorites from the many regional areas of Mexico, as well as from his own family. Pescado Yucateco—filet of fish broiled with sliced onions and garlic and laced with spices—is a Mayan favorite, and a very popular item.

"Contrary to general belief, Mexican cooking is not necessarily hot. In many dishes the seasonings are subtle and the range of dishes goes far beyond the popular tacos, tamales, and enchiladas," says Mrs. Olga Flores, manager.

La Margarita is open seven days a week for lunch, as well as seven nights a week for dinner. Strolling guitarists serenade every evening, while mariachi musicians are a mid-week special.

6319 Dempster
Morton Grove

SANGRÍA

6 tablespoons lemon juice	Dry red wine
6 tablespoons sugar	6 maraschino cherries
1½ cups orange juice	6 slices orange for garnish
Club soda	

1. Combine the lemon juice, sugar, and orange juice. Pour the mixture into 6 (12-ounce) glasses filled with ice. Add club soda until three-fourths of each glass has been filled. Pour dry red wine to the top of each glass.
2. Decorate each glass with a maraschino cherry and a slice of orange.

SOPA DE AJO
Garlic Soup

10 cloves garlic	Salt and pepper to taste
3 tablespoons butter	6 eggs
2 tablespoons flour	2 tablespoons chopped parsley
1½ quarts beef or chicken stock, strained	3 tablespoons crumbled Jack cheese
3 drops Tabasco sauce	

1. Mash the garlic as finely as possible. Melt the butter in a heavy saucepan over medium heat; add the garlic and flour and sauté until the garlic is soft.
2. Add the stock. Bring to a boil; reduce heat and simmer 15 minutes.
3. Strain and return the stock to heat. Add the Tabasco sauce, salt, and pepper. Return to a boil.
4. Crack the eggs one at a time into a small bowl and carefully slide each into the boiling soup. Cook until the eggs are poached.
5. Ladle into bowls, 1 egg per bowl. Sprinkle with parsley and crumbled cheese.

GUACAMOLE

2 ripe avocados, peeled and seeded

1 large tomato, peeled and chopped

1 small green hot pepper, minced

1 large onion, minced
Salt to taste

¼ cup oil, lemon juice, or dry white wine
Corn tortilla chips for dipping

Mash the avocados. Combine all ingredients except the tortilla chips in a large bowl, mixing well. Taste and adjust seasonings. Chill until ready to serve.

Leave the two avocado pits in the guacamole until ready to serve. This prevents discoloration.

GARNACHAS
Fried Tortillas with Tomato Sauce, Refried Beans and Cheese

½ onion, minced

½ green pepper, chopped

1 large tomato, peeled, seeded, and chopped

3 tablespoons vegetable oil

12 tortillas

2 cups cooking oil
FRIJOLES REFRITOS
Shredded longhorn cheese

1. Sauté the onion, green pepper, and tomato in the 3 tablespoons oil until tender.
2. Cut the tortillas in quarters and brown in deep oil.
3. Spread each tortilla chip with the refried beans and then the tomato sauce.
4. Place on a cookie sheet and sprinkle the cheese over. Place in a hot oven or under the broiler until the cheese has melted.

FRIJOLES REFRITOS

1 pound dried pinto beans	2 tablespoons corn oil
1 onion, chopped	Grated hard cheese
1 ham hock, or ½ pound bacon	

1. Soak the beans overnight in 3 times their volume of water.
2. In the morning, drain and cook them with the onion, ham hock or bacon, and water to cover. Continue cooking until the beans are tender, 1½ to 3 hours.
3. Heat the oil in a heavy skillet. Mash the beans with a potato masher and add to the oil. Sprinkle with grated cheese.

CHILES RELLENOS

12 small bell peppers	Salt
2 (3-ounce) packages cream cheese)	2 cups oil for deep-frying
	1 cup all-purpose flour
6 eggs	SAUCE

1. Slit the peppers at the lower end and remove the seeds and pulp, but leave the stem on. Boil in water until tender; drain.
2. Slice the cream cheese and stuff each pepper with pieces of cheese.
3. Separate the eggs. Beat the whites until they form soft peaks, then add the yolks and continue beating until uniform and fluffy. Lightly salt the egg batter.
4. Heat the oil in a skillet to 375°. Roll the peppers in flour, dip in the egg batter, and fry on both sides until golden brown. Drain on paper toweling.
5. Serve covered with Sauce.

SAUCE

2 tablespoons corn oil	¼ teaspoon oregano
¼ cup chopped onion	Salt and pepper
1½ cups tomato sauce	

Heat the oil in a large skillet over medium heat. Sauté the onion until soft. Reduce heat and add the tomato sauce, oregano, salt, and pepper; mix well. Simmer for 5 minutes.

ASADO DE PLÁTANOS
Steak with Fried Bananas

2 *pounds round steak*	½ *cup water*
¼ *cup corn oil*	2 *tablespoons sugar*
Salt and pepper	4 *cooking bananas*
1 *onion, chopped*	*(plantains)*
½ *cup sherry*	

1. Fry the steak in 3 tablespoons oil over high heat until both sides are well browned.
2. Sprinkle with salt, pepper, and chopped onion. Pour in the wine and water. Cover tightly and simmer 45 minutes or until a fork passes easily through the meat.
3. In another pan, heat the remaining 1 tablespoon oil; sprinkle in the sugar and allow to turn a golden color.
4. Cut the bananas in half lengthwise and add to the skillet. Remove from heat when the bananas are well browned on both sides. Serve the meat cut in portions and bathed in its own sauce, with the bananas on the side.

SOPA DE ARROZ

1 *cup uncooked rice*	2 *cloves garlic, mashed*
2 *tablespoons corn oil*	*Salt and pepper*
1 *small onion, chopped*	2½ *cups chicken stock*

1. Sauté the dry rice in oil over low heat for 5 minutes.
2. Add the onion and garlic and sauté another 5 minutes.
3. Add salt and pepper to taste and stir in the stock.
4. Cover tightly and finish cooking over your lowest heat for 30 to 40 minutes or until the stock is absorbed.

This is a sopa seca, *or dry soup.*

CALABACITAS CON CREMA
Squash and Cream Sauce

1 pound young, tender summer squash	1 pint fresh cream Salt and pepper
4 bell peppers	1 tablespoon finely grated
1 small onion	Parmesan cheese (optional)
2 tablespoons butter	

1. Slice the summer squash and peppers as thinly as possible and finely chop the onion.
2. Melt the butter in a ceramic casserole dish over medium heat. Add the vegetables. Cover and cook until tender, about 12 minutes.
3. Stir in the cream and sprinkle with salt and pepper. Heat until hot. If desired, add a tablespoon of finely grated Parmesan cheese.

FLÁN

6 tablespoons sugar	3 cups milk, scalded and cooled
3 tablespoons water	
6 eggs, beaten	Dash of salt
1 teaspoon vanilla extract	¼ cup sugar
1 teaspoon grated lemon zest	

1. Place the sugar and water in a small, heavy saucepan. Cook over medium heat until the sugar begins to turn a light golden color.
2. Using pot holders and a wooden spoon, carefully pour the sugar syrup into a 2-quart ring mold. Using the pot holders, rotate the mold so that the caramel coats the bottom and sides before it hardens. Set aside to cool.
3. Place 2" of water in a deep pan large enough to hold the ring mold. Place in oven and preheat to 350°.
4. In a large mixing bowl, combine the eggs, vanilla, lemon zest, cooled milk, salt, and sugar. Pour the mixture into the prepared mold.
5. Place the mold into the larger pan with water. Bake 50 minutes or until set. Remove from the pan of water and allow to cool. Refrigerate.
6. To serve, unmold on a serving platter.

Dinner for Four

Pizza Soup

Fedelini Pesto

Veal Parmesan

Peach Flambé

Wine:

With the Pesto—*Joseph Phelps Sauvignon Blanc, 1979*
or for a very special occasion
Château Margaux Pavillon Blanc, 1976

With the Veal—*Chianti Clàssico, Castello di Uzzano, 1974*

Larry Aronson, Owner

MY PIE

Larry Aronson, founder and owner of My Pie, has more than a touch of the baker's blood in him. His father had a hearth-oven bakery on the North Side, and Larry grew up in an atmosphere of authentic home-country cooking, surrounded by the old ethnic neighborhoods. At fifteen he opened a successful hot-dog stand; at college, he was fraternity steward and campus pizza man. It might seem he was a natural for the restaurant trade, but that wasn't what happened next. Larry got a job as teletype operator at the local branch of a New York securities brokerage. Within four years he was sales manager, and another seven saw him become a partner in charge of central regional sales. Four years later he left the business. Why? "I didn't enjoy it anymore," he says.

In the meantime he had set up My Pie, and it was this enterprise he threw himself into. My Pie "is not just a pizza business, but my philosophy of life," he states. "I look at the opportunity to succeed as a benefit of this country." To take advantage of this opportunity, Larry calls upon a set of high standards and some strongly held opinions.

"I grew up with the traditions of the turn of the century. It's not hard to make good food if you go back to the basics. We only use natural ingredients and have fresh products every day. We don't use tomato sauce or paste—we use fresh, crushed Italian plum tomatoes, because they have a sweet, fruity flavor." He guards against *bruciore*—heartburn, in Italian— by using skim-milk mozzarella, which he gets from a farm in Wisconsin; local meatcutters make his sausage to specification, which includes the use of roast-cut meat rather than the usual fat trimmings. The pizza dough is kneaded by hand, with the flour added a bit at a time. "You know it's ready when you poke your finger into it and it comes out clean. I watched them make this for eight years before they'd let me do it," he says of his father's bakery.

6568 North Sheridan Road
Rogers Park

PIZZA SOUP

3 quarts Beef Stock (see index), cold	¼ pound mushrooms, sliced
¼ pound ground beef	1 small onion, diced
¼ pound bulk Italian sausage	½ green pepper, diced
16 thin slices peperoni	¼ cup grated Parmesan cheese
1½ cups TOMATO SAUCE (see next page)	¼ cup bread crumbs
	¼ cup dry red wine

1. Place the beef stock in a 4-quart stock pot. Roll the ground beef and, separately, the sausage, into ½" balls. Add to the stock, along with the peperoni, Tomato Sauce, mushrooms, onion, and green pepper. Bring slowly to a boil, reduce heat to a light roll, and cook for 1½ hours.
2. Add the Parmesan cheese, bread crumbs, and wine; simmer for 10 minutes. Serve hot.

By placing the pot off center over the burner, you can get a rolling motion that stirs the liquid, eliminating the need for stirring by hand.

TOMATO SAUCE

1 (28-ounce) can Italian plum tomatoes	½ teaspoon oregano
1 tablespoon sugar	¾ teaspoon salt
½ teaspoon basil	¼ teaspoon pepper
	2 tablespoons Wesson oil

Mince the tomatoes. Place the tomatoes with their juice in a saucepan; add the remaining ingredients and stir with a wooden spoon. Gently heat to bubbling, then reduce the heat and simmer 10 minutes.

This recipe makes enough sauce for both the Pizza Soup and the Veal Parmesan which follows.

FEDELINI PESTO

⅓ cup pine nuts
½ cup extra virgin olive oil
½ cup freshly grated
   Parmesan cheese
2 large cloves garlic, peeled
1 teaspoon salt

¼ teaspoon black pepper
2 cups loosely packed fresh
   basil leaves
½ pound fedelini #1,
   preferably Agnesi brand

1. Place the pine nuts, olive oil, Parmesan cheese, garlic, salt, pepper, and basil in a blender or a food processor fitted with a steel blade and blend until finely minced. Use a spatula to scrape the sauce into a sauté pan or chafing dish. Set aside.
2. Bring 3 quarts salted water to a boil. Add the fedelini, separating it as you drop it into the water. Stir once or twice during the first minute. Cook al dente (Agnesi fedelini takes about 4½ minutes; other brands take longer).
3. Warm the pesto mixture over medium heat for about 2 minutes. Drain the fedelini and add to the pesto pan. Toss lightly until coated. Serve immediately.

If the pine nuts are not very fresh and crisp, place under the broiler until they color slightly to freshen up. Pine nuts are available at gourmet food stores.

VEAL PARMESAN

2 cups Tomato Sauce, approximately (see Pizza Soup recipe)
¾ teaspoon salt
¼ teaspoon pepper
¾ cup bread crumbs
4 (¾") veal filets mignons, butterflied (preferably Provimo veal)

Flour for dredging
2 eggs, beaten
¼ pound butter, clarified
¼ cup Wesson oil
1 large clove garlic, minced
8 slices mozzarella cheese
¼ cup grated Parmesan cheese

1. Place the tomato sauce in a saucepan over low heat to warm.
2. Mix the salt, pepper, and bread crumbs in a bowl.
3. Press the butterflied veal filets with the flat side of a heavy knife to about ¼" thick. Dredge in flour, dip to coat well in the beaten eggs, and dredge in the bread crumbs to coat evenly and thoroughly. As the filets are breaded, lay out on waxed paper. If possible, allow the breading to set for 30 minutes.
4. Preheat oven to 450°.
5. Heat the clarified butter and oil with the garlic in a large sauté pan over medium-high heat. When hot, add the breaded veal and sauté on both sides until golden brown. Drain on paper toweling.
6. Place the veal in a baking pan. Cover each portion with 2 slices mozzarella cheese. Ladle a generous amount of tomato sauce over each, sprinkle with the grated Parmesan cheese, and bake in preheated oven for 10 minutes or until the cheeses are melted.
7. Place under broiler to glaze the cheese. Serve immediately.

Note: To clarify butter, it is handy to have a long-handled pot in the shape of a narrow cylinder. Place the butter in it and melt gently over low heat. When melted, skim the foam off the top. Carefully pour the butter oil into another container, leaving the white solids in the bottom of the first pot. Discard the foam and solids; the clear liquid is clarified butter.

It would be easiest to have your butcher butterfly the veal filets, but it is not difficult to do at home: with a very sharp knife, slice through the middle of the filet to within ¼" of cutting all the way through. Open out like a book and press flat.

PEACH FLAMBÉ

⅓ cup fresh orange juice
⅓ cup fresh lemon juice
⅓ cup sugar
8 peach halves, Freestone
  or Elberta
1 cup whipping cream, chilled

½ teaspoon vanilla extract
½ cup powdered sugar
1 ounce Triple Sec liqueur
4 large scoops vanilla ice cream
½ cup toasted almonds
  (optional)

1. Combine the orange and lemon juices with the sugar. If the peaches are canned, drain well. Place in a narrow container and add the juice mixture. Place in the refrigerator for 4 to 6 hours.
2. Drain the peach halves and place in a saucepan. Bring to a boil, reduce heat to a simmer, and poach for about 8 minutes (4 minutes if using canned peaches) or until cooked but not mushy.
3. Place the whipping cream in a chilled bowl. With a chilled whisk, beat until it begins to thicken. Add the vanilla extract and powdered sugar and continue to whip until the peaks hold. Place in a pastry bag with a plain or fluted tip.
4. Sprinkle the Triple Sec over the peaches and ignite with a match. Allow to flame for a few seconds, then begin spooning the pan liquid over the peaches until the flame dies out.
5. Place 2 peach halves in each dessert dish. Top with a scoop of ice cream and a tablespoon of the pan syrup. Pipe the whipped cream over decoratively; garnish with toasted almonds if desired.

The flambé may be done at tableside for an extraordinary effect: while the peaches are cooking, warm the Triple Sec in a small pan. Take the peaches, ice cream, whipped cream, and the pan with the Triple Sec to the table. Flame the Triple Sec, pour over the peaches, and proceed to assemble as directed. Of course, use caution whenever working with an open flame.

94TH AERO SQUADRON

Dinner for Six

Bongo Bongo Soup

Farmhouse Salad with Honey-Mustard Dressing

Farmhouse Chicken

Broccoli au Beurre

Cheesecake

Wine:

Pouilly-Fuissé

Specialty Restaurants Corporation, Owner
Richard K. Chee, General Manager
Sidney Garber, Chef

94TH AERO SQUADRON

The Ninety-Fourth Aero Squadron restaurant is patterned after the French farmhouse that served the illustrious unit of the American Expeditionary Force as headquarters during the first world war. David Tallichet, now chairman of the board of the Specialty Restaurant Corporation, had developed an interest in the chivalric first age of military aviation after serving as a flier in a later war. In 1959 he was able to share his passion with the dining public by opening a restaurant that combines the interest of a museum, the romance of a glamorous era, and the satisfaction of good country cooking.

Prime steaks, fresh salads, and American and French country dishes are offered among reminders of those bygone days. Sandbags, Sopwith Camel aeroplanes, and old posters share space with farm tools and furniture of the era. The lobby is filled with memorabilia of the Great War and the aces of the day, including Eddie Rickenbacker and John Newman Hall. From the moment you cross the wooden bridge and pass Checkpoint Charlie, you are thrust into the world of the boys who flew the planes with the hat-and-ring insignia—the Ninety-Fourth Aero Squadron.

1070 South Milwaukee Avenue
Wheeling

BONGO BONGO SOUP

½ pound fresh spinach, or
¼ pound frozen spinach,
thawed

¼ pound plus 4 tablespoons
butter

½ cup all-purpose flour

1 quart whipping cream
30 freshly shucked oysters
Salt and pepper to taste
8 drops Tabasco sauce
1 teaspoon Worcestershire
sauce

1. Wash the spinach thoroughly if using fresh. Chop and steam in the water clinging to the leaves for about 1 minute. Remove from heat and set aside.
2. Prepare a roux by melting ¼ pound butter in a large, heavy saucepan. Whisk in the flour and simmer 4 minutes, whisking constantly. Do not allow to brown.
3. Gradually whisk in the cream. Very slowly heat to a light simmer. Do not allow to boil.
4. Heat the remaining 4 tablespoons butter in a skillet. Sauté the oysters until they begin to fall apart. With the back of a wooden spoon, break into small bite-size pieces.
5. Stir the oysters, spinach, and seasonings into the thickened cream. Serve warm.

94TH AERO SQUADRON

FARMHOUSE SALAD WITH HONEY-MUSTARD DRESSING

1 *head Boston lettuce, torn into bite-size pieces*	2 *large tomatoes, cut into wedges*
½ *head romaine lettuce, torn into bite-size pieces*	12 *mushrooms, sliced*
1 *cucumber, sliced*	½ *head cauliflower, cut into florets*
6 *stalks celery, diced*	*HONEY-MUSTARD DRESSING*
1 *medium-size zucchini, thinly sliced*	

Arrange the vegetables on 6 chilled salad plates. Drizzle the dressing over when ready to serve.

HONEY-MUSTARD DRESSING

½ *cup mayonnaise*	*Salt to taste*
1 *tablespoon vegetable oil*	2 *teaspoons finely diced onion*
1 *tablespoon honey*	
1 *tablespoon white vinegar*	2 *teaspoons chopped parsley*
1 *tablespoon sugar*	
1 *tablespoon prepared mustard*	

Place the mayonnaise in a small bowl. Beat in the oil. Thoroughly mix in the remaining ingredients. Refrigerate at least 1 day.

FARMHOUSE CHICKEN

1½ cups salad oil
½ cup vinegar
2 tablespoons lemon juice
½ teaspoon salt
½ teaspoon black pepper
2 tablespoons rosemary
6 boneless chicken breasts, with skin

6 thin slices smoked ham
6 slices Monterey Jack cheese
3 tablespoons butter
12 mushrooms, sliced
2 cups demi-glace

1. Combine the salad oil, vinegar, lemon juice, salt, pepper, and rosemary in a bowl. Whisk well, add the chicken breasts, and marinate overnight.
2. Preheat the broiler. Drain the chicken and lay out on a baking sheet. Broil about 6 to 8 minutes per side or until cooked through.
3. Place the breasts skin side up. Lay a ham slice over each. Top with a slice of cheese and return to the broiler until the cheese is melted.
4. Melt the butter in a skillet over medium-high heat. Add the mushrooms and sauté until soft.
5. In a saucepan, heat the demi-glace to a light simmer. Stir in the mushrooms.
6. Place the chicken on a serving platter. Ladle the sauce over and serve.

BROCCOLI AU BEURRE

1 large head broccoli
5 tablespoons butter, melted

Salt and pepper to taste

Trim the leaves and thick stems off the broccoli. Cut the florets into bite-size pieces and steam until tender, 10 to 15 minutes. Remove to a serving bowl. Toss with butter. Add salt and pepper to taste and serve immediately.

CHEESECAKE

2½ pounds cream cheese,
    room temperature
½ cup whipping cream
¼ cup flour
2 cups sugar
1 tablespoon fresh lemon juice
1 teaspoon pure vanilla
    extract

3 tablespoons Curaçao
    or other orange liqueur
5 eggs, lightly beaten
2 egg yolks, lightly beaten
CRUST

1. Preheat oven to 550°.
2. Place the cream cheese in a large mixing bowl. Beat 10 minutes at low speed, scraping the sides of the bowl occasionally.
3. In a separate bowl, mix the cream, flour, sugar, lemon juice, vanilla extract, and liqueur. Beat the mixture into the cheese for 5 minutes.
4. Beat in the eggs and yolks. Continue beating until the mixture is light and fluffy.
5. Pour into the Crust and bake in preheated oven until the top is a light golden brown, 5 to 7 minutes. Rotate the pan 180° and bake an additional 4 minutes. Turn the oven off, open the door, and let the cake cool 20 minutes in the oven.
6. Set the oven to 250°, close the door, and bake 1 hour and 20 minutes. Cool in the oven as above before refrigerating.

94TH AERO SQUADRON

CRUST

¼ cup all-purpose flour
2½ cups crushed vanilla
    cookies (such as Lorna
    Doone)
½ cup sugar

1 tablespoon grated lemon
   zest
¼ pound butter, melted
3 egg yolks, well beaten

Combine the ingredients in a mixing bowl. Pat into the bottom and sides of a 10" spring-form pan.

Pine Yard

Dinner for Four

Fried Rice

Crispy Beef

Spicy Shrimp

Chicken with Walnuts

Abalone Soup

Wine:
Chenin Blanc

Stella and Eric Hsish, Owners
Erich Hsish, Head Chef

PINE YARD

In China, a pine yard is a special place, green and peaceful. With this image in mind, Eric and Stella Hsish have created a restaurant with an atmosphere of tranquility and comfort. Both Stella and Eric came to the United States from Taiwan to study accounting at the University of Missouri. While in school, their hobby was cooking their native dishes for fellow students. Many of the recipes they prepared are unique, having been developed by Eric's family, who are restaurateurs in Taiwan.

After graduation eight years ago, they agreed to continue their hobby by opening a restaurant. On the advice of a friend, they decided to settle in Evanston near Northwestern University. The town's college atmosphere and cosmopolitan population have been very conducive to their innovative cooking style. As the chef, Eric is constantly trying new recipes, adding them to the menu after a test period only if they meet his clients' approval.

In Eric's opinion, good food starts with the best raw materials. "I only accept the finest and the freshest quality ingredients. My purveyors know I will refuse anything that is not up to my standards. I am very particular," he adds. Further, all the dishes at the Pine Yard are made to order; nothing languishes on a steam table.

The Pine Yard's marketing policy is no less unique than the menu: the consistently excellent quality of the food does the talking for them. "Our business has grown through word of mouth only," Stella says. "We have never advertised. Our satisfied customers do the advertising for us."

924 Church Street
Evanston

FRIED RICE

¼ cup peanut oil
2 eggs, lightly beaten
3 green onions, chopped
3 cups cooked rice
2 tablespoons soy sauce

1 cup cubed or shredded
cooked pork
1 small carrot, grated
1 cup cooked green peas, warm

1. Heat 2 tablespoons of the oil in a wok or heavy skillet. Stir-fry the eggs until cooked but still moist, breaking up clumps. Reserve.
2. Heat the remaining oil in the wok and stir-fry the green onions until tender. Mix in the rice, soy sauce, pork, and carrot, stirring well after each addition. Add the eggs, stir well, and remove to a serving dish. Sprinkle the peas over and serve.

CRISPY BEEF

¾ pound beef flank steak
3 tablespoons soy sauce
2 tablespoons red wine
1 teaspoon sesame oil
1 slice ginger root, minced
1 egg, lightly beaten
3 tablespoons cornstarch
3 tablespoons all-purpose
flour

1 teaspoon baking powder
2 cups peanut oil
2 tablespoons toasted sesame
seeds
2 large tomatoes, cut
in wedges
½ cup trimmed parsley sprigs

1. Slice the beef into thin strips across the grain of the meat. Mix the soy sauce, wine, sesame oil, and ginger. Marinate the beef in the mixture 10 minutes.
2. Combine the egg, cornstarch, flour, and baking powder in a small bowl. Allow to stand 15 minutes.
3. Heat the peanut oil to 375° in a wok or heavy skillet. Remove the beef from the marinade and dip in the egg mixture to coat. Deep-fry ½ cup at a time until golden brown. Drain on paper toweling.
4. Arrange on a serving plate. Sprinkle with sesame seeds; arrange the tomato wedges and parsley sprigs decoratively around the beef.

By allowing the batter to stand for 15 minutes, the flour absorbs the liquid and will make a thicker batter. All batter, including those for pancakes, crêpes, etc., should follow this procedure.

SPICY SHRIMP

1 pound medium-size shrimp
2 tablespoons rice wine or dry sherry
1 egg white
3 tablespoons cornstarch
2 cups peanut oil
2 slices ginger, minced
2 cloves garlic, minced
3 green onions, chopped

2 tablespoons hot bean sauce or Tabasco sauce
4½ tablespoons ketchup
2 tablespoons soy sauce
1 tablespoon vinegar
½ teaspoon salt
½ cup Chicken Stock (see index)

1. Shell and devein the shrimp, leaving the tails on. Wash and drain.
2. Combine the wine, egg white, and 1 tablespoon cornstarch. Add the shrimp and toss.
3. Heat the oil to 375° in a wok or heavy skillet. Fry the shrimp just until opaque; remove and drain on paper toweling.
4. Remove all but about 3 tablespoons oil from the wok. Add the ginger, garlic, and green onions and stir-fry until tender.
5. Dissolve the remaining cornstarch in the chicken stock. Add to the wok with the remaining ingredients and the shrimp. Stir-fry until the sauce thickens slightly. Serve hot.

Hot bean sauce is a thick sauce made from beans and spicy seasonings. It is found in Chinese groceries.

CHICKEN WITH WALNUTS

1 large whole chicken breast, skinned and boned
½ teaspoon salt
1 teaspoon sugar
2 tablespoons cornstarch
3 tablespoons soy sauce
4 dried black mushrooms
1 cup shelled walnuts

2 cups peanut oil
3 cloves garlic, minced
3 stalks celery, sliced
1 large onion, sliced
1 cup sliced bamboo shoots
¼ cup Chicken Stock (see index)

1. Shred the chicken meat. Combine the salt, sugar, cornstarch, and soy sauce. Marinate the chicken meat in this mixture for 20 minutes.
2. Soak the dried mushrooms in warm water for 15 minutes. Drain, trim off the tough ends, and thinly slice the mushrooms.

3. Place the walnuts in a small pan. Cover with cold water, bring to a boil, and continue boiling 3 minutes. Drain.
4. Heat the oil to 375° in a wok or heavy skillet. Deep-fry the walnuts until lightly browned. Drain on paper toweling.
5. Remove all but 3 tablespoons of the oil. Add the garlic and stir-fry until lightly browned. Add the marinated chicken meat and stir-fry until opaque, about 1 minute.
6. Add the celery, onion, bamboo shoots, and mushrooms. Stir-fry until tender-crisp, about 2 minutes.
7. Stir in the chicken stock. Cook until the sauce thickens slightly.
8. Remove to a large platter. Garnish with the browned walnuts.

Dried black mushrooms can be found in Chinese groceries.

ABALONE SOUP

4 cups Chicken Stock (see index)	1 small carrot, grated
1 slice ginger, grated	½ cup chopped celery
1 green onion, chopped	½ cup sliced canned abalone
	1 teaspoon salt

Bring the chicken stock to a boil. Add the ginger, onion, carrot, and celery. Simmer for 15 to 20 minutes. Add the abalone and salt to taste. Allow to heat and ladle into individual soup bowls.

The soup may be prepared ahead of time and reheated when ready to serve.

According to Chinese custom, soup is served at the end of the meal, after all the entrées and just before dessert. For this menu, a simple dessert of fresh fruit is recommended.

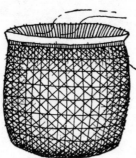

R.J. GRUNTS

Dinner for Six

Herring Salad

Tomato Soup

Cheezy Chicken with Mornay Sauce

Glazed Carrots

Vegetable Pasta Salad

Pecan Pie

Wine:

Soave

Lettuce Entertain You Enterprises, Owner

R.J. GRUNTS

When a restaurant can offer a relaxed atmosphere, reasonable prices, and an eclectic menu, it is providing a good deal. If it can do all that and also have very good food, it is a bonanza. And when an entire group of varied restaurants under a single management can do it, it is incredible. In the last decade, Lettuce Entertain You Enterprises has wrought such a miracle in Chicago, and one of the latest waves of their magic wand has created R.J. Grunts in Glenview.

Catering to both the dieter and the gourmand, the menu includes everything from filet mignon, ribs, and duck, to chimichangas, peanut-butter-and-duck sandwiches (in season), to the ubiquitous but ever-lovable hamburger and cottage fries. Dominating everything, like a vast cornucopia of nature's bounty, is a multi-tiered, multi-item salad bar with every conceivable goody, including crunchies and munchies for your salad, shrimp, herring, and pasta salads, the freshest sliced fruits in season, and a variety of toppings. This salad bar includes thirty-five items during the day; the number grows to forty-five for the evening meal.

"At Grunts we cater to the neurotic compensation of eating in a contemporary wood, glass, and brass atmosphere," the management boasts. What they should add is that your neuroses never had it so good. It is fine food—with a chuckle.

1615 Milwaukee Avenue
Glenview

HERRING SALAD

1 pound herring, packed in
  wine, drained
3 medium-size cucumbers
½ pound firm tomatoes

2 medium-size green
  peppers, seeded
1 large Spanish onion

1. Cut the herring into bite-size pieces; place in a large serving bowl.
2. Peel the cucumbers. Cut in half lengthwise and scoop out the seeds with a spoon. Finely slice all the vegetables.
3. Mix the herring and sliced vegetables thoroughly. Chill until ready to serve, tossing again before serving.

This salad is outstanding for a patio lunch in the summer.

TOMATO SOUP

3 cups peeled and chopped
  fresh tomatoes
½ cup water
1 medium-size onion, thinly
  sliced
2 sprigs parsley, minced

3 tablespoons butter
3 tablespoons all-purpose
  flour
3 cups half-and-half
  Salt and pepper
2 cups sliced mushrooms

1. Combine the tomatoes, water, onion, and parsley in a heavy saucepan. Simmer for 20 minutes.
2. Melt the butter in a 3 or 4-quart saucepan over medium heat. Whisk in the flour until it is absorbed and continue stirring for 5 minutes. Add the half-and-half in a slow, steady stream. Bring the mixture to a boil, reduce heat to a simmer, and continue cooking for 5 minutes, stirring continuously. The mixture will thicken slightly.
3. Stir in the tomato mixture. Season to taste with salt and pepper. Pour into soup bowls and garnish with sliced mushrooms.

Canned tomatoes can be used. Substitute the tomato liquid for the water.

This soup can be chilled and served cold. Serve in a tall glass with a celery stick.

CHEEZY CHICKEN WITH MORNAY SAUCE

MORNAY SAUCE
1 *pound egg noodles, cooked according to package directions*
6 *tablespoons margarine*
6 *skinless, boneless chicken breasts*

¾ *pound mozzarella cheese, sliced*
Freshly grated Parmesan cheese
Chopped parsley

1. Spread a thin layer of Mornay Sauce to cover the bottom of a casserole. Place the cooked pasta over the sauce.
2. Heat the margarine in a heavy skillet. Sauté the chicken on both sides until cooked through but still tender, 6 to 8 minutes. Place over the pasta.
3. Ladle a thin layer of Mornay Sauce over all and cover with sliced mozzarella cheese. Place under preheated broiler until the cheese is melted and lightly golden.
4. Sprinkle with Parmesan cheese, garnish with parsley, and serve.

If possible, always use freshly grated Parmesan cheese—you will be surprised at the difference in taste.

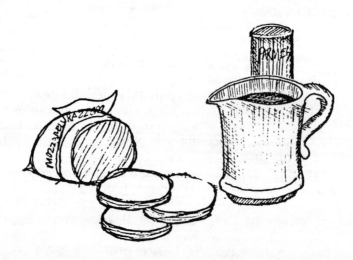

MORNAY SAUCE

¼ pound butter
1 medium-size onion, chopped
5 tablespoons all-purpose flour
3 cups milk

¼ cup Chicken Stock (see index)
½ teaspoon white pepper
½ teaspoon garlic powder
1 small carrot, grated

1. Heat the butter in a large saucepan over medium heat. Sauté the onion until soft.
2. Whisk in the flour until absorbed. Simmer, whisking constantly, for 3 to 5 minutes. Mix in the milk, chicken stock, white pepper, garlic powder, and grated carrot. Continue to simmer until the sauce is thick and creamy.

GLAZED CARROTS

1 pound carrots, peeled, thinly sliced
¼ cup granulated sugar

3 tablespoons butter, room temperature

1. Cook the carrots, covered, in boiling water until tender. Drain.
2. Melt the sugar in a heavy skillet over medium heat, stirring, until lightly caramelized.
3. Mix in the butter. Add the cooked, drained carrots and stir over the heat until the carrots are glazed, about 4 to 5 minutes.

VEGETABLE PASTA SALAD

1 green pepper, seeded	2 tablespoons white vinegar
1 Spanish onion	2 tablespoons salad oil
6 stalks celery	1 teaspoon salt
½ cup whole pimientos	½ teaspoon white pepper
¼ pound peperoni	½ teaspoon powdered garlic
1 pound small pasta shells, cooked al dente	1 teaspoon Worcestershire sauce
1 cup mayonnaise	½ cup stuffed green olives

1. Finely chop the pepper, onion, celery, and pimientos.
2. Thinly slice the peperoni. Toss with the chopped vegetables in a deep salad bowl. Add the cooked pasta shells to the chopped vegetables, mixing well.
3. In a small bowl, thoroughly combine the mayonnaise, white vinegar, salad oil, salt, white pepper, powdered garlic, and Worcestershire sauce. Pour over the salad and toss well.
4. Chill until ready to serve. Garnish with the green olives before serving.

R.J. GRUNTS

PECAN PIE

3 eggs
¼ cup light brown sugar,
   firmly packed
1⅓ cups light corn syrup
¾ tablespoon vanilla extract

¼ cup flour
1 cup pecans
1 (10") graham cracker
   pie shell

1. Preheat oven to 325°.
2. Combine all ingredients except the pie shell, mixing thoroughly by hand. Spread evenly in the shell.
3. Bake in preheated oven for 1 hour. Allow to cool to room temperature before serving.

ARMENIAN RESTAURANT

Dinner for Six

Raw Kibbee

Hummos

Taboule

Sautéed Chicken Breasts

Rice Pilaf

Burma

Wine:

Cabernet Sauvignon

Leon and Marj Demerdjian, Owners and Chefs

SAYAT NOVA

Sayat Nova, a seventeenth-century Armenian troubadour, would feel at home in the charming Des Plaines restaurant named for him. From the table-sized, white-stuccoed alcoves, to the music drifting through the dining room, the ambiance is Middle Eastern and the food is authentic.

"I came to the United States twenty-three years ago," owner Leon Demerdjian relates, "after being raised in Lebanon, where my parents sought refuge in 1915. Following a short stint in a typically American-style restaurant, my brother and I decided to introduce Chicago to the food of Armenia.

"Although in general we use the same basic ingredients as the Greeks, Turks, and Arabs," Demerdjian goes on, "our proportions vary. Lemon juice, olive oil, garlic, yogurt, and filo pastry are as familiar to the Armenian as to the Athenian. But there are some non-common elements as well. Instead of the Greek passion for oregano, we use an herb called sumac. Combined with the different balance of seasonings, it adds up to a very unique taste.

"And, finally, ours is a healthy cuisine," Demerdjian concludes. "My menu, rich in vegetables, homemade yogurt, cracked wheat, and lean meats, is a nutritionist's delight." The diner will not quarrel with that, but as one contentedly bites into a fragile baklava dessert, filled with nuts and coated with a delicate sugar syrup, he undoubtedly concludes that it is food for the palate as well.

20 West Golf Road
Des Plaines

SAYAT NOVA

RAW KIBBEE

1 cup fine bulghur wheat	1 teaspoon salt
½ cup ice-cold water	¼ teaspoon pepper
1 pound sirloin steak, well trimmed	Olive oil
	Lemon wedges
½ cup chopped parsley	Pita bread
½ cup chopped onion	

1. Soak the bulghur wheat in the ice water for 10 minutes.
2. Grind the sirloin 4 times in a meat grinder. Add to the wheat with half the parsley and half the onion. Season with the salt and pepper and knead about 5 minutes.
3. Form the mixture into a large patty on a serving plate. Make a depression in the center with your thumb. Drizzle the olive oil into the depression.
4. Garnish with the remaining parsley and onion and the lemon wedges. Serve with warm pita bread.

Ask your butcher to remove all the fat and membranes from the sirloin; he may also grind it for you. Dip your hands in ice water during the kneading to prevent the mixture from getting too sticky.

Fine bulghur wheat may be found in many grocery stores and nearly any Middle-Eastern food store.

HUMMOS

1 (28-ounce) can chickpeas (garbanzo beans)
⅓ cup tahini
¼ cup lemon juice
2 cloves garlic, crushed

Salt and pepper to taste
2 tablespoons olive oil
¼ cup chopped parsley
Dash of paprika
Pita bread

1. Drain the chickpeas, reserving the juice. Place the chickpeas, tahini, lemon juice, garlic, salt, and pepper in a blender and process until smooth. The consistency should be similar to cooked oatmeal; if too dry, add some of the reserved chickpea juice.
2. Place in a serving dish, drizzle with olive oil, and garnish with parlsey and paprika.

Tahini is a sesame paste that may be found in most grocery stores. Hummos can be prepared a day ahead, re-mixed, and served.

TABOULE

¼ cup fine bulghur wheat
¼ cup olive oil
⅔ cup chopped parsley
¼ cup chopped onion
⅓ cup chopped green pepper
1½ cups chopped fresh tomatoes
Salt and pepper to taste

1 to 2 tablespoons chopped dried mint
Juice of 1 lemon, or about ⅓ cup
½ head romaine lettuce, torn into bite-size pieces

1. Place the wheat in a mixing bowl and cover with the olive oil.
2. Add, as you chop them, the parsley, onion, green pepper and to-matoes. Mix in the salt, pepper, mint, and lemon juice. Refrigerate at least 15 minutes.
3. Serve on a platter decorated with romaine lettuce.

Be sure to use a good grade of olive oil; it is crucial to a recipe such as this.

SAUTÉED CHICKEN BREASTS

⅓ cup olive oil
⅓ cup lemon juice
1 teaspoon sumac
4 to 6 cloves garlic, crushed
6 chicken breasts

2 Spanish onions
4 green peppers
¼ pound plus 3 tablespoons butter
Salt and pepper to taste

1. Combine the olive oil, lemon juice, sumac, garlic, and 1 teaspoon salt.
2. Skin and debone the chicken breasts and cut into 2" by 2" pieces. Marinate overnight in the olive oil/lemon juice mixture.
3. Chop the onions and green peppers into 1" by 1" pieces. Melt the butter over high heat in a large, heavy frying pan, preferably of stainless steel. Add chicken pieces, onions, and green peppers all at once and sauté for about 6 to 7 minutes, stirring frequently. Season to taste with salt and pepper.

Ground sumac may be found in most Middle-Eastern grocery stores.

RICE PILAF

½ cup thin chinese egg noodles
⅓ cup butter
2 cups uncooked long-grain rice

4 cups Chicken Stock (see index)

1. Sauté the noodles in the butter in a large pan until browned.
2. Add the uncooked rice and stir to coat with butter.
3. Add the stock and simmer, stirring occasionally, until the stock is absorbed and the rice is tender, about 18 minutes.
4. Cover and let set for a few minutes before serving.

Water and/or chicken bouillon may be substituted for the chicken stock.

BURMA

You will need a wooden dowel with a diameter of ½" for this recipe. A suitably sized curtain rod may be substituted.

4 cups ground walnuts	¼ pound plus 4 tablespoons
¾ cup sugar	unsalted butter, melted
8 sheets filo dough	SUGAR SYRUP

1. Preheat oven to 375°.
2. Combine the walnuts and sugar.
3. Cut the filo sheets in half. Working with 1 half-sheet at a time, lay out on the working surface and brush liberally with butter.
4. Place the dowel across the sheet, one-quarter of the way from one end. Sprinkle ¼ cup of the walnut mixture in a line just to the inside of the dowel. Fold the end of the sheet over the dowel and press lightly to cover the walnuts. Roll up the sheet around the dowel, leaving about ¾" unwrapped.
5. Carefully slip the dowel out of the cylinder of dough. Form into a spiral with the unwrapped 'lip' toward the inside. Pinch the exposed end back into the spiral.
6. Place about 1 teaspoon of the walnut mixture in the center of the spiral.
7. Repeat this procedure for the remaining filo. Place on a baking sheet and drizzle with remaining preheated butter. Bake in preheated oven for 20 to 25 minutes or until golden brown.
8. Spoon Sugar Syrup over. Allow to cool before serving.

Makes 16 burmas.

Cover the unused portion of the filo dough with a damp towel to keep it from drying out while you work.

SAYAT NOVA

SUGAR SYRUP

2 cups sugar	2 tablespoons lemon juice
1 cup water	1 tablespoon grated lemon zest

Combine the ingredients in a small saucepan. Bring the mixture to a boil, reduce heat to simmer, and cook 5 to 6 minutes. Strain before using.

Serve with Armenian demi-tasse coffee and Armenian Ararat brandy.

Le Titi de Paris

Dinner for Four

Saucisson de Faison en Croûte

Cream of Mushroom Soup

Chicken and Lobster with Watercress and Spinach Sauce

Parsnips

Strawberries à la Crème

Wine:

Vouvray, Château Moncontour, 1979

Pierre Pollin, Owner and Chef

LE TITI DE PARIS

From the moment one enters the front hall and sees the brocaded walls and dark woods, and experiences the elegant manner in which patrons are seated, expectations of exquisite dining begin to take root in the imagination. The dimmed lighting, fresh flowers, and fine china suggest an intimate rite of the table, full of pleasures both secret and shared. Pierre Pollin, owner-chef of Le Titi de Paris, is devoted to the authenticity and attention to detail of the Parisian restaurants in which he was trained. This attention extends outward from the kitchen to the dining room: nearly as as much care is given to the setting and service of a meal as to the cuisine itself, the raison d'être of the whole establishment.

Back in the kitchen, a forty-gallon stock pot is always bubbling. The refrigerators bulge with the bones, marrow, and vegetables needed to feed it. "We use no flour bases for our sauces," Pollin states. "We depend instead upon stock reductions. My soufflés achieve their height only on the basis of their airy egg whites. I also stress the use of fresh fruit in my sauces and desserts. The emphasis is on lightness, which is in tune with my customers' desire to avoid the heavy foods that would spoil their lifestyles."

Because *la nouvelle cuisine* does not translate well to mass production, Pollin keeps his restaurant small and intimate. It is his feeling that there is no need to sacrifice his insistence on quality to meet demands for quantity. As a result, dinner at Le Titi de Paris is similar to a meal at Monsieur Pollin's home.

2275 Rand Road
Palatine

SAUCISSON DE FAISAN EN CROÛTE

¼ pound pheasant breast,
    boned and skinned
¼ pound chicken breast,
    boned and skinned
1 teaspoon salt
2 eggs
1 cup whipping cream
2 ounces pork sausage

½ teaspoon pepper
    (approximately)
1 tablespoon pine nuts
½ cup cooked spinach, drained
1 sheet puff pastry
GREEN PEPPERCORN
    SAUCE (see next page)

1. Grind the pheasant and chicken separately with a meat grinder or food processor. If using a meat grinder, grind twice; if using a food processor, grind with the steel blade until finely minced.
2. With a mixer or food processor, combine the chicken, two-thirds of the pheasant, the salt, and 1 egg. When well mixed, add the cream gradually and blend in.
3. Mix in the pork sausage, remaining pheasant, pepper, and pine nuts by hand. Set the mixture aside.
4. Preheat oven to 375°.
5. Squeeze the spinach dry and chop medium-finely. Set aside.
6. Roll the puff pastry into a rectangle approximately 8" by 12", ⅛" thick. Place half the sausage mixture down the center of the pastry, leaving about 2" on either end.
7. Form a shallow trough down the center of the sausage mixture. Fill with the chopped spinach and cover with the remaining sausage mixture. Re-form into an even log shape.
8. Fold the ends of the puff pastry over. Bring the sides together at the top and double-fold to enclose the meat. Lightly beat the remaining egg and brush the seams with it to seal. Place in a baking pan, seam side down, and brush with egg.
9. Bake in preheated oven for 20 minutes or until the pastry is golden. Slice and serve with hot Green Peppercorn Sauce.

Substitute dark chicken meat if pheasant is not available. Pine nuts and prepared puff pastry are available in gourmet shops and many supermarkets.

GREEN PEPPERCORN SAUCE

1 cup roast beef drippings	½ teaspoon lemon juice
1½ cups beef bouillon	Salt and pepper to taste
2 tablespoons cognac or brandy	3 tablespoons butter, room temperature
3 tablespoons green peppercorns, well drained	1 cup whipping cream

1. Place the drippings, bouillon, and cognac in a 1-quart saucepan over medium-high heat. Bring to a boil, reduce heat, and simmer until reduced to 2 cups.
2. Crush the peppercorns with the back of a spoon or the flat of a knife. Add the peppercorns, lemon juice, salt, and pepper to the bouillon mixture. Remove the pan from heat.
3. Stir in the butter, piece by piece. Stir in the cream.

If you don't happen to have roast beef drippings on hand, just use another cup of bouillon in their place.

CREAM OF MUSHROOM SOUP

¾ pound fresh mushrooms	4 cups Chicken Stock (see index)
5 to 6 tablespoons butter	White pepper to taste
1 small onion, minced	1 cup light cream
3 tablespoons all-purpose flour	

1. Slice enough mushrooms to make ¾ cup; reserve for garnish. Mince the remainder.
2. Melt the butter in a 2 or 3-quart saucepan. Add the onion and sauté over medium heat, stirring until wilted.
3. Mix in the minced mushrooms, dust with the flour, and continue cooking until the mushrooms are soft. Stir occasionally.
4. Slowly stir in the stock and pepper. Bring the mixture to a boil, reduce heat to simmer, and continue cooking 5 minutes.
5. Blend in the cream. Ladle the soup into individual bowls. Garnish with sliced mushrooms.

CHICKEN AND LOBSTER WITH WATERCRESS
AND SPINACH SAUCE

5 ounces lean veal, ground and chilled
½ teaspoon salt
⅛ teaspoon white pepper
½ cup whipping cream
2 whole chicken breasts, boned
4 to 6 large spinach leaves, washed, tough stems removed

2 teaspoons raisins
½ lemon
2 (5-ounce) lobster tails, shelled
¼ cup unsalted butter
2 tablespoons oil
2 to 3 cups cooked white rice
WATERCRESS AND SPINACH SAUCE (see next page)

1. Combine the veal, salt, and pepper with a food processor or electric mixer. When well mixed, add the cream gradually and continue to mix until light and smooth. Chill.
2. Preheat oven to 375°.
3. Place the chicken breasts skin side down between 2 sheets of plastic wrap on a cutting board. Pound with the flat side of a meat mallet to about ¼" thick, spreading the meat to the outside as you pound.
4. Remove the top sheet of plastic wrap. Spread the veal mousse over. Lay the spinach leaves over in a single layer and sprinkle 1 teaspoon raisins on each piece.
5. Squeeze the lemon juice over the lobster tails. Place each lengthwise on a chicken breast. Roll each breast up into a small log. Tuck in the ends and tie the packages with string, as for a rolled roast.
6. Melt the butter in a medium-size ovenproof sauté pan over medium-high heat. Add the oil; heat until the butter foams. Add the chicken rolls and brown on all sides, about 5 minutes.
7. Transfer to preheated oven for 15 minutes. Let stand at least 5 minutes after baking. Remove the strings and slice ¼" thick. Arrange over cooked white rice and serve with Watercress and Spinach Sauce.

WATERCRESS AND SPINACH SAUCE

1 cup spinach, washed
   and trimmed

1 cup watercress, washed
   and trimmed

3 tablespoons unsalted
   butter

3 tablespoons chopped
   shallots

½ cup dry white wine

2 tablespoons cream sherry

2 cups Chicken Stock
   (see index)

1 cup whipping cream

2 teaspoons cornstarch
   (as needed)

Salt and pepper to taste

1. Plunge the spinach and watercress in boiling water. When the leaves turn bright green, remove and place in cold water. Drain and squeeze to remove excess moisture. Chop very finely and mix to form a thick paste.
2. Melt 2 tablespoons butter in a heavy 1-quart saucepan over medium heat. Add the shallots and sauté until golden.
3. Add the wine and sherry. Raise the heat to high and cook until the liquid is completely evaporated.
4. Immediately add the chicken stock. Cook until reduced to ¼ cup.
5. Add the cream and allow to boil for 1 minute, stirring constantly. Remove from heat and add the remaining tablespoon of butter, bit by bit, whisking to combine.
6. Add the spinach and watercress paste, whisking to combine. The sauce should have the consistency of thick gravy; if it does not, dissolve up to 2 teaspoons cornstarch in a little cold water, stock, or cream. Whisk into the sauce and bring to a boil. Reduce heat and whisk until thickened.
7. Season to taste with salt and pepper.

PARSNIPS

1 *pound parsnips*   2 *cups peanut oil*

1. Scrape the parsnips with a knife to clean. Thinly slice on the diagonal and cut into strips.
2. Heat the oil to 375°. Fry the parsnips, a few pieces at a time, until golden brown. Drain on paper toweling. Serve hot.

STRAWBERRIES A LA CRÈME

1½ *pints strawberries*   ¾ *teaspoon vanilla extract*
 ¾ *cup whipping cream, chilled*   ¼ *cup confectioners' sugar*

1. Cut the strawberries in half lengthwise. Place in a mixing bowl.
2. Whip the cream until it begins to thicken. Sprinkle with the vanilla extract and confectioners' sugar. Continue whipping until soft peaks form.
3. Gently stir the cream into the berries. Spoon carefully into 4 glass goblets, taking care not to drip down the sides of the glasses. Refrigerate until ready to serve.

TOWER
GARDEN & RESTAURANT

Dinner for Four

Trout Filet Marguery

Spinach Salad à la Tower Garden

Chicken à la Tarragoneza

Black Forest Torte

Wine:

With the Chicken—a California Fumé Blanc, or
Pinot Chardonnay, France or California

With the Torte—a California late harvest Johannisberg Riesling, or
a Rhein Auslese

Reinhard Barthel, Manager

TOWER GARDEN AND RESTAURANT

Although its doors were first opened in 1934, the Tower Garden and Restaurant has come into its own only since 1968. Under the tutelage of Swiss-trained Chef Reinhard Barthel, the productions of the kitchen have come to fulfill and exceed the charm of the setting. The Garden Room's summery oranges and greens, skylights and hanging plants, play host to such visual and palatial delights as imported Dover sole in beurre noir sauce and roast duckling with brandied orange slices and grapes, served over raisin dressing.

Barthel's influence is equally felt in the large selection of wines available, the result of his expert taste and curiosity. "Because I am especially interested in sharing my knowledge, I have helped to found several flourishing wine clubs, as well as expanding my own collection," he explains. "Gourmets have always been interested in wines and have delighted in tasting many varieties, considering this an essential part of any meal. This viewpoint is now shared by many Americans, and our cellar is a tribute to that growing enthusiasm."

9925 Gross Point Road
Skokie

TROUT FILET MARGUERY

2 *shallots, minced*
⅓ *cup sliced mushrooms*
½ *cup raw shrimp, shelled and split in half*
1 *tablespoon butter*
1 *cup white wine*
1 to 2 *teaspoons chives*
1 *cup BÉCHAMEL SAUCE*
1 *small onion, sliced*

1 *bay leaf*
Juice of 1 lemon
Salt and pepper to taste
4 to 5 *cloves*
4 *(4 to 6-ounce) trout filets, skinned*
1 *tablespoon HOLLANDAISE SAUCE (see* Chicken à la Tarragoneza *recipe)*

1. Sauté the minced shallots, mushrooms, and shrimp in the butter. Add ¼ cup wine, the chives, and Béchamel Sauce. Stir over heat to warm.
2. In a large saucepan, place the onion, bay leaf, lemon juice, salt, pepper, cloves, remaining wine, and water to cover the trout. Bring to a boil, add the trout filets, and poach 4 minutes or until the flesh begins to flake when pressed. Drain and place on a serving platter.
3. Stir the Hollandaise Sauce into the warm Béchamel mixture. Spoon over the filets and serve.

BÉCHAMEL SAUCE

3 tablespoons butter	Pinch of pepper
2 tablespoons flour	Pinch of salt
¼ teaspoon minced onion	Pinch of nutmeg
Pinch of thyme	1½ cups milk

1. Melt 2 tablespoons butter in a small saucepan. Add the flour and cook over medium heat for 3 minutes, stirring constantly. Do not allow to brown.
2. Add the remaining butter, onion, and seasonings. Cook, stirring constantly, until the onion is tender but not browned.
3. Gradually add the milk, stirring well to prevent lumps. Reduce heat and simmer 15 to 20 minutes. Strain before using.

If it is necessary to hold this sauce for any length of time, a film of butter over the surface will prevent the formation of a skin.

SPINACH SALAD A LA TOWER GARDEN

⅓ cup sugar	1 pound spinach, washed and drained
1 tablespoon English dry mustard	
¼ cup cider vinegar	2 hard-cooked eggs, chopped
1 cup salad oil	Bacon bits

1. Blend the sugar, dry mustard, and cider vinegar. Add the oil gradually while whisking vigorously to a heavy consistency.
2. Remove the tough stems of the spinach and tear large leaves to bite size. Toss with dressing to taste.
3. Top with chopped eggs and bacon bits.

Colman's mustard is excellent in this recipe.

CHICKEN A LA TARRAGONEZA

1 *cup wild rice*
1 *cup flour*
  Salt
  Pepper
6 *chicken breasts, boned*
¼ *pound plus 1 tablespoon butter*

HOLLANDAISE SAUCE
(see next page)
½ *teaspoon tarragon leaves*

1. Wash the wild rice thoroughly and place in a saucepan. Pour over enough boiling water to cover. Cover with a tight-fitting lid and let stand until cool. Drain; repeat 3 more times.
2. Season the flour with salt and pepper to taste. Dredge the chicken in the flour, shaking to remove excess flour.
3. Melt ¼ pound butter in a large skillet over medium heat and sauté the chicken until golden brown on both sides, about 25 minutes.
4. Finish preparing the wild rice by seasoning with about 1 tablespoon each of salt and butter and rewarming in the oven or in a double boiler.
5. To serve, place the chicken breasts on beds of wild rice. Top each with Hollandaise Sauce to taste, sprinkle with crushed tarragon leaves, and brown under a preheated broiler.

HOLLANDAISE SAUCE

3 large egg yolks
1 tablespoon water
¼ pound plus 2 tablespoons
   butter, softened

¾ teaspoon lemon juice
¼ teaspoon salt
¼ teaspon pepper
   Dash of cayenne

Whisk the egg yolks and water to a thick froth in a heavy saucepan over very low heat, or in a double boiler over barely simmering water. Add the butter tablespoon by tablespoon, whisking constantly, until the mixture thickens. Season with lemon juice, salt, pepper, and cayenne.

Makes 1 cup.

BLACK FOREST TORTE

1 cup sugar
½ cup butter, room
   temperature
6 eggs, separated, room
   temperature
1 cup cake flour
⅓ cup milk
½ cup plus 1 tablespoon cocoa
½ teaspoon baking soda
½ teaspoon baking powder

½ cup plus 1 tablespoon
   kirschwasser
1 pint whipping cream,
   chilled
1 (17-ounce) can tart
   cherries, including juice
2 tablespoons cornstarch
½ cup shaved semisweet
   chocolate

1. Preheat oven to 350°.
2. Grease and flour 2 (8") layer cake pans.
3. Beat ¾ cup sugar and the butter in a large mixing bowl until light and fluffy. Beat in the egg yolks, one at a time. Slowly beat in the cake flour, milk, 6 tablespoons cocoa, baking soda, and baking powder.
4. Beat the egg whites with a wire whisk or rotary beater until soft peaks form. Fold into the batter.
5. Spread the mixture evenly into the prepared pans. Bake in preheated oven for 35 minutes or until a knife or cake tester inserted in the center comes out clean. Remove from oven and place on a wire rack to cool.
6. Using a serrated knife, split one layer in half. Sprinkle all 3 layers with kirschwasser, using about 3 tablespoons per layer.

7. Whip the cream until soft peaks form. Add the remaining ¼ cup sugar and 3 tablespoons cocoa and whip until the peaks hold. Place in a pastry bag.

8. Combine the cherries with their juice and the cornstarch in a saucepan over medium heat. Stir continuously until thick. Remove from the heat. Select 12 choice cherries to reserve for decoration.

9. Place the thick layer of cake on a dessert plater. Pipe a fairly thick ring of chocolate cream around the top edge. Spoon enough of the cherries in sauce to fill the center of the cream ring.

10. Top with a thin layer of cake. Pipe a double ring of chocolate cream around the edge. Fill the center with the remaining cherries in the sauce.

11. Top with the remaining thin cake layer. Cover the top and sides of the torte with the remaining chocolate cream. Sprinkle with shaved chocolate. Place the reserved 12 cherries in a ring around the top rim. Refrigerate until ready to serve.

The Village Smithy

Dinner for Six

Broiled Salmon with Dill Sauce

Spinach Salad with Mustard Dressing

Chicken Dijon

Steamed Artichokes

Apple Brown Betty

Wine:

With the Salmon—Chalone Vineyard Chardonnay, 1978

With the Chicken—Rosent Semillon Blanc, 1979

With the Brown Betty—Schramsberg Cremant, 1978

Bill Lepman, Owner

VILLAGE SMITHY

Bill and Barbara Lepman, the owners of the Village Smithy, have blended their love of domestic wines and their interest in American cooking to develop a restaurant that is truly a celebration of America. They chose their location because of its historical significance: the old Glencoe blacksmith shop. The Lepmans have maintained the nineteenth-century atmosphere through effective use of enlarged original photographs, pewter serving dishes, and turn-of-the-century artifacts. Within this setting they offer American regional specialties and wine selections.

"I feel that an appreciation of American food is growing, as well-known authorities begin to explore the richness and diversity in cooking styles that exist in our own country," Bill observes. This must be gratifying to him, as he continues his experimentation with recipes old and new, deriving from times and places as diverse as colonial Boston and contemporary California. The menu at the Village Smithy is in constant evolution as new recipes are perfected and turned over to the staff of able cooks.

368 Park Avenue
Glencoe

BROILED SALMON WITH DILL SAUCE

6 (4 to 5-ounce) salmon filets	3 tablespoons butter, melted
Dry white wine	DILL SAUCE

1. Preheat broiler. Place the salmon filets skin side down in a broiler-proof shallow baking dish. Add enough wine to half-immerse the filets.
2. Brush the tops of the filets with butter. Broil very close to the heat just until the flesh flakes when pressed.
3. Place on a heated platter. Spoon Dill Sauce over and serve immediately.

DILL SAUCE

1 cup dry white wine	Salt
¼ cup white vinegar	White pepper
¼ small onion, minced	1 tablespoon minced fresh
¾ cup whipping cream	dill weed
¾ pound unsalted butter, softened	

1. In an enameled saucepan, heat the wine, vinegar, and onion to a boil. Reduce heat and simmer until the liquid is reduced to about 1 tablespoon.
2. Add the cream and continue to simmer until reduced to 2 tablespoons. The sauce should now have the consistency of thin mayonnaise. Remove from heat.
3. Stir in bits of softened butter until incorporated. Season to taste with salt and white pepper.
4. When ready to serve, stir in the fresh dill weed.

SPINACH SALAD WITH MUSTARD DRESSING

1 egg	½ teaspoon freshly ground
1 cup cottonseed or	coarse black pepper
sunflower oil	½ pound spinach, washed
2 tablespoons fresh	thoroughly
lemon juice	4 hard-cooked eggs, minced
¼ cup Dusseldorf mustard	¼ pound bacon, cooked crisp
¾ teaspoon Worcestershire	and crumbled
sauce	

1. Beat the egg with a mixer at medium speed until light. Add the oil slowly, mixing until incorporated. Slowly add the lemon juice, mustard, Worcestershire sauce, and pepper, blending well.
2. Remove the tough stems from the spinach. Place in a mixing bowl. Add dressing to taste, the minced eggs, and crumbled bacon. Toss gently.

CHICKEN DIJON

½ pound butter	3 tablespoons Dijon mustard
¼ cup chopped chives	1½ teaspoons Lawry's
¼ cup chopped parsley	seasoned salt
2 tablespoons minced garlic	1½ teaspoons paprika
1 cup fresh bread crumbs	6 boneless chicken breasts

1. Whip the butter until tripled in volume. Add the remaining ingredients except the chicken breasts and continue whipping until well combined.
2. Turn the butter mixture out onto a large sheet of waxed paper. Shape into a log about 1½" in diameter. Wrap well in the waxed paper and freeze at least 1 hour or until ready to use.
3. Bake the chicken breasts at 350° for 15 minutes or until cooked through. Remove from oven.
4. Preheat the broiler. Place the chicken breasts in individual ramekins. Slice 12 silver-dollar-size pieces off the frozen roll of Dijon butter and place 2 slices over each chicken breast. Broil until the butter has melted and the bread crumbs in it are crisp. Serve immediately.

If you wish to serve the chicken breasts with the skin on, baste with a small amount of melted butter before baking. The skin may be crisped under the broiler for a few moments before adding the Dijon butter.

Dijon butter may be served over a variety of meats and other foods. This recipe will leave you with a surplus, which should be kept frozen until use.

STEAMED ARTICHOKES

6 artichokes   1 lemon

1. Remove the artichoke stems. Cut 1½" off the top of each artichoke with a heavy, sharp knife. Snip the tips off the leaves with scissors.
2. Cut the lemon into 6 round slices. Place the artichokes in a large steamer over boiling water; place 1 lemon round over each artichoke. Cover tightly and steam for 40 to 45 minutes, or until the leaves pull off easily.

Serve with your favorite dip.

APPLE BROWN BETTY

¼ pound butter
3 cups fresh bread crumbs
2 pounds tart apples, peeled and sliced
½ teaspoon cinnamon

½ cup brown sugar
½ cup apple juice
Sweetened whipped cream or vanilla ice cream (optional)

1. Preheat oven to 375°.
2. Melt the butter and mix in the crumbs. Press two-thirds of the crumbs into the bottom and sides of a 9" by 9" by 2" baking dish.
3. Combine the apples, cinnamon, brown sugar, and apple juice. Pour into the prepared baking dish and distribute the apple slices evenly. Sprinkle with the remaining crumbs.
4. Cover the dish and bake in preheated oven for 20 to 25 minutes. Uncover and continue baking for another 25 minutes or until brown and crispy.
5. Cut into portions and serve topped with whipped cream or ice cream if desired, on rimmed dessert plates or in bowls.

Yu-Lin's Chinese Dumpling House

Dinner for Six

Deep-Fried Eggplant Pastry

Onion Cakes

Hot and Sour Soup

Sweet and Sour Yellow Pike

Chicken in a Nest
or
Kung Pao Chicken

Shredded Beef with Green Peppers

Dry-Cooked String Beans

Wine:
Wang Fu

Yu-Lin Hsuieh, Owner

YU-LIN'S CHINESE DUMPLING HOUSE

There was a time in the dark, dimly remembered culinary past when the term 'Chinese food' in America meant Cantonese. Then, to the delight of gourmets and connoisseurs, the spicier flavors of Mandarin cuisine were introduced. Their favorable reception insured a permanent place in America's dining habits, not only to Mandarin cooking but to all of China's regional cuisines. For Yu-Lin Hsuieh, this emergence from the dark ages heralded the best possible time to enter the restaurant business. With her husband, she opened a small establishment on Chicago's far north side, moving to her present Highland Park location a few years later.

Yu-Lin's emphasizes the tastes of northern China without discarding the culinary treasures of Canton. Among the specialties of this cosy, warm restaurant is a dish called the Firepot, served on request. A gleaming pot of chicken broth is brought to the table over hot coals. Platters of artfully arranged lamb, chicken , spinach, green onions, and assorted other vegetables are placed around the pot. Diners cook the food in the broth, as for a fondue, then savor it with the accompaniment of several pungent sauces. The meal is concluded by sipping the now flavorful broth.

Another house specialty is evident in the establishment's name. "The restaurant is named for the dumplings that are so abundant in the diet of the North," Yu-Lin explains. "I make my own dumpling dough and fillings. Guests particularly like the pot stickers that are so enjoyable as a mild appetizer before a meal that might also include the fiery taste of Kung Pao Chicken and the milder Shredded Beef with Green Peppers." She concludes with a summation of her service philosophy: "Balance and harmony are essential to Chinese life. I want my customers to feel relaxed and content when they leave my restaurant."

1636 Old Deerfield Road
Highland Park

DEEP-FRIED EGGPLANT PASTRY

1 (1½-pound) eggplant	3¼ cups plus 2 tablespoons oil
1 tablespoon dried shrimp	¼ teaspoon salt
5 green onions	1 tablespoon sugar
6 ounces ground pork or beef	1½ tablespoons vinegar
1 tablespoon plus 1 teaspoon chopped ginger	1 tablespoon sherry
2 tablespoons soy sauce	1 tablespoon soybean paste or Hoisin sauce
2 tablespoons sesame oil	1 tablespoon chopped fresh garlic
½ cup all-purpose flour	1 tomato, sliced
1 cup plus ½ teaspoon cornstarch	1 small cucumber, sliced
2 eggs	Chopped parsley

1. Slice the ends off the eggplant and cut in half lengthwise. Leaving the skin on, cut into ½" slices. Stand each slice on its skin side and partially slice through the middle, almost as though butterflying, to make a sandwich-like pocket for stuffing.
2. Soak the dried shrimp in water until soft, about 10 minutes. Drain and chop together with 3 green onions. Mix the shrimp and chopped green onions with the ground meat, 1 teaspoon ginger, 1 tablespoon soy sauce, and 1 tablespoon sesame oil. When mixed well into a stiff paste, stuff into the eggplant pockets.
3. Combine the flour, 1 cup cornstarch, the eggs, 1 cup water, and 3 tablespoons oil into a smooth paste. Set aside.
4. Separately, combine the salt, sugar, remaining 1 tablespoon soy sauce, vinegar, 2 tablespoons water, remaining ½ teaspoon cornstarch, sherry, and remaining 1 tablespoon sesame oil. Set aside.
5. Heat 3 cups oil to 375° in a wok. Dip the stuffed eggplant slices into the flour paste to coat well and deep-fry until golden brown. Remove and drain.
6. When all the eggplant has been fried, allow the oil to come back up to heat and re-fry the slices for 10 seconds each. Drain again and place on a serving platter.
7. Chop the remaining 2 green onions. In a saucepan, combine the onions, soybean paste, garlic, remaining chopped ginger, remaining 3 tablespoons oil, and the reserved vinegar/sherry mixture. Bring to a boil and pour over the fried stuffed eggplant.
8. Garnish with the sliced tomato and cucumber and the chopped parsley. Serve immediately.

YU-LIN'S CHINESE DUMPLING HOUSE

China offers a great range of dried foodstuffs: vegetables, fruit, poultry, and sea-food. Most of these, including the dried shrimp used here, must be softened before using by soaking in water.

Soybean paste is made from fermented soybeans, flour and salt. Both it and Hoisin sauce may be purchased at Chinese groceries.

ONION CAKES

4 cups all-purpose flour	3 green onions, chopped
1¼ cups boiling water	1½ teaspoons salt
¼ cup cold water	
1 cup plus about 3 tablespoons salad oil	

1. Place the flour in a deep bowl. Pour the boiling water over and mix with chopsticks without stopping for 3 minutes. Add the cold water and knead the dough until smooth. Cover and let rest 30 minutes.
2. Turn the dough out on a lightly floured board. Divide into 8 equal portions and roll each piece into a ball. With a rolling pin, roll each ball into a 10" circle.
3. Spread about 2 teaspoons oil over each circle. Divide the chopped green onions and the salt over each and roll up tightly.
4 Coil each of the long, thin rolls into a spiral shape. Pull the outside end into a thin strand; tuck into the center of the spiral. Press each spiral to flatten and roll out to ¼" thick.
4. For each cake, heat 2 tablespoons oil in a sauté pan over medium heat. Cook, one at a time, on one side for 2 minutes, then carefully turn and cook the other side for about 1 minute or until crisp and golden, adding another teaspoon of oil if necessary. Drain on paper toweling. Repeat for remaining cakes.
5. When all cakes are cooked, cut into bite-sized wedges and serve.

HOT AND SOUR SOUP

6 dried black mushrooms
2 tablespoons dried tree
   ear mushrooms
6 cups Chicken Stock
   (see index)
¼ pound beef or pork
½ cup tofu
2 tablespoons plus ¼
   teaspoon salt
1 egg white
1 (4-ounce) can bamboo
   shoots, shredded

2 green onions, chopped
3 tablespoons cornstarch
3 slices ginger, peeled
   and minced
2 eggs, lightly beaten
1 teaspoon vinegar
1 teaspoon black vinegar
1 teaspoon black pepper
1 tablespoon sesame oil

1. Soak the black mushrooms and tree ear mushrooms in hot water for 15 minutes to soften. When soft, remove any tough stems and discard. Shred the mushrooms with a knife or cleaver.
2. Bring the chicken stock to a boil in a wok or large pot. Slice the meat into thin strips and chop into shreds. Slice the tofu into 1½" by ¾" strips.
3. Combine the shredded meat, ¼ teaspoon salt, and egg white, mixing well. When the stock comes to a boil, reduce heat to simmer and add the mushrooms, tofu, meat mixture, bamboo shoots, green onions, and ginger. Mix the cornstarch with ¼ cup cold water and stir into the soup.
4. Return to a boil and remove from heat. Slowly stir in the eggs.
5. Place the vinegars, pepper, remaining salt, and sesame oil in a serving bowl. Add the hot soup and serve immediately.

Black mushrooms, tree ear mushrooms, and black vinegar may be purchased at Chinese groceries. Tofu, or soybean curd, is found in the produce departments of most supermarkets.

SWEET AND SOUR YELLOW PIKE

1 (1½ to 2-pound) yellow
  pike, cleaned and scaled,
  head and tail on
2 tablespoons salt
1 cup white wine
2 eggs
1 cup all-purpose flour

¼ cup cornstarch
1 cup water
1 teaspoon baking soda
6 cups peanut oil for
  deep-frying
SWEET AND SOUR SAUCE
(see next page)

1. Rinse the fish under cold running water. Lay on a board. Cut through to
   the backbone just behind the head and gill fin on each side. Place the
   fish on its back and slit to—but not through—the backbone from head
   to tail. Open the fish out and remove the accessible bones, leaving the
   head and tail on.
2. Cut 3 slits lengthwise down each side, about ¼" deep. Place in a flat pan
   and marinate 10 minutes in the salt and wine.
3. In a mixing bowl, mix the eggs, flour, cornstarch, water, and baking
   soda until smooth. Heat the oil in a wok to 375°, or almost smoking. As
   the oil comes up to heat, dip first the fish head and then the remainder
   in the batter to coat well. Holding the fish by the head and tail, carefully
   lower into the hot oil. Fry until golden brown, turning as necessary. Remove from the oil, drain, and place on a serving platter.
4. Drain the oil from the wok, leaving about 2 tablespoons. Reheat over
   medium heat and add the Sweet and Sour Sauce. Cook for about a minute and a half. Spoon over the fish, removing the cinnamon sticks,
   and serve.

*To test the oil temperature for deep-frying, stand a clean, dry chopstick in the
oil. If bubbles form around the end, the oil is about 375° and ready for frying.*

YU-LIN'S CHINESE DUMPLING HOUSE

SWEET AND SOUR SAUCE

2 sticks cinnamon
Juice of 1 lemon
1 white onion, sliced
2 slices pineapple, cut into
  1" pieces
½ green pepper, diced
2 tablespoons raisins

½ cup white vinegar
1 tablespoon cooking wine
6 tablespoons sugar
¼ cup ketchup
1 cup water
1 teaspoon salt

Combine the ingredients in a saucepan and bring to a boil. Reduce heat and simmer 3 minutes, adding more water if necessary.

The sweet-sour balance may be adjusted to taste by adding more sugar or vinegar.

YU-LIN'S CHINESE DUMPLING HOUSE

CHICKEN IN A NEST

1 *pound boneless chicken breasts, skin removed*
1 *egg white*
2 *tablespoons cornstarch*
1 *tablespoon dark soy sauce*
2 *tablespoons light soy sauce*
1 *tablespoon white wine or saké*
¼ *teaspoon salt*
½ *teaspoon sugar*
¼ *teaspoon black pepper*
½ *teaspoon sesame oil*
¼ *pound cellophane noodles (bean threads)*

4 to 6 *cups oil*
⅓ *pound fresh spinach or other greens, chopped*
3 *tablespoons diced green onions, whites only*
1 *tablespoon sliced ginger*
10 *mushrooms, sliced*
¼ *cup sliced water chestnuts*
¼ *cup chopped bamboo shoots*
½ *small carrot, thinly sliced*
1 *cup diced (½") green pepper*

1. Dice the chicken into ½" pieces. Mix the egg white, 1½ tablespoons cornstarch, and the dark soy sauce and marinate the chicken in the mixture for 30 minutes.
2. Combine the light soy sauce, the remaining ½ tablespoon cornstarch, the wine, salt, sugar, pepper, and sesame oil in a small bowl. Set aside.
3. Soak the noodles in warm water for 5 minutes to soften. Drain well and press into a strainer to form a nest shape.
4. Heat the oil to 375° in a wok over high heat. Place a second strainer over the noodles in the first, to keep in a nest shape, and deep-fry for a few seconds until expanded and opaque, but not browned. Carefully remove the nest from the strainers and drain.
5. Remove all but about 2 cups oil from the wok and reserve. Return the wok to heat and deep-fry the chicken meat until opaque. Drain on paper toweling.
6. Remove all but about 2 tablespoons oil from the wok. Return to heat and stir-fry the spinach (or other greens) about 1½ minutes. Remove and set aside.
7. Return about ¼ cup oil to the wok. Return to heat and stir-fry the green onions, ginger, mushrooms, water chestnuts, carrot, and green pepper for about 1 minute. Return the chicken meat and stir-fry about 1 minute more. Add the reserved light soy sauce seasoning mixture and stir until it comes up to heat.
8. Place the fried greens on a serving platter. Set the noodle nest in the greens, fill with the chicken mixture, and serve.

KUNG PAO CHICKEN

2 pounds chicken breasts
1 egg
1½ teaspoons cornstarch
3 tablespoons white wine or saké
1 tablespoon vegetable oil
1 teaspoon salt
3 cups peanut oil for deep-frying
2 dried hot red peppers, seeds removed, thinly sliced

2 green onions, sliced ¼"
3 slices ginger, peeled and minced
2 tablespoons soy sauce
1 teaspoon sugar
1 tablespoon hot pepper oil
1 teaspoon sesame oil
½ cup peanuts

1. Skin and bone the chicken and dice into ½" cubes. Mix the egg, cornstarch, 1 tablespoon wine, vegetable oil, and salt in a bowl. Marinate the chicken for 30 minutes.
2. Heat the peanut oil to 375° in a wok over high heat. Deep-fry the chicken for about 2 minutes or until barely cooked through; drain.
3. Remove all but about 2 tablespoons oil from the wok. Return to heat and stir-fry the peppers, green onions, and ginger, until the onions are tender. Return the chicken to the wok and stir-fry about 10 seconds, or until heated through. Add the soy sauce, remaining wine, sugar, hot pepper oil, salt, and sesame oil; stir-fry about 20 seconds.
4. Reduce heat to medium-low and add the peanuts. Simmer about 1 minute and serve.

If your skin is sensitive, wear rubber gloves when handling the hot red peppers.

Hot pepper oil is available at Chinese groceries and some supermarkets. If you are not familiar with it, start with less than the recommended 1 tablespoon and adjust to taste—it is very hot.

SHREDDED BEEF WITH GREEN PEPPER

1 pound beef flank steak	3 green peppers
2 tablespoons soy sauce	1 green onion
2 tablespoons red wine	1½ cups peanut oil
1½ tablespoons cornstarch	3 slices ginger, peeled and minced
2 teaspoons salt	1 teaspoon sugar
2 tablespoons salad oil	
1 egg	

1. Thinly slice the beef across the grain. Slice again in 1½″ lengths to shred. Combine the soy sauce, wine, cornstarch, 1 teaspoon salt, salad oil, and egg in a bowl. Marinate the beef in the mixture for 1 hour.
2. Halve the green peppers and remove the seeds and membranes. Thinly slice crosswise; reserve.
3. Cut the green onion in 1½″ lengths. Thinly slice each section to shred.
4. Heat the peanut oil to 375° in a wok over high heat. Place the shredded beef in a strainer and dip in the hot oil for 1 or 2 seconds to sear. Drain on paper toweling.
5. Remove all but about 3 tablespoons of the oil. Return the wok to heat and stir-fry the green onion and ginger until the onion is soft. Add the shredded peppers, sugar, and remaining salt; stir-fry about 1 minute. Return the beef to the wok and stir-fry about 1 minute more. Serve.

When stir-frying, all ingredients should be prepared beforehand and should be at arm's length.

DRY-COOKED STRING BEANS

1¼ pounds small, tender string beans (1½")	2 tablespoons salt
2 tablespoons dried shrimp	1 teaspoon sugar
¼ cup salted vegetables or salted cucumber	¼ cup Chicken Stock (see index)
3 cups peanut oil	1 tablespoon soy sauce
3 ounces ground pork or beef	½ tablespoon vinegar
2 slices ginger, peeled and minced	1 teaspoon sesame oil
	1 green onion, chopped

1. Remove the tips and strings from the beans. Soak the dried shrimp in warm water for 10 minutes. Wash the salted vegetables thoroughly under cold water and drain. Chop the shrimp and vegetables into small pieces.
2. Heat the peanut oil to 375° in a wok over high heat. Deep-fry the beans, one cupful at a time, for 3 or 4 minutes or until wrinkled, and drain. Drain the oil from the wok and reserve.
3. Return the wok to medium heat. Return the beans to the wok and scorch until brown, stirring constantly. Remove beans and set aside.
4. Return 2 tablespoons oil to the wok. When hot, add the ground meat and ginger and stir-fry until the meat is cooked, about 3 minutes. Add the dried shrimp and vegetables and stir-fry another 3 minutes. Add the salt, sugar, chicken stock, soy sauce, and the cooked beans. Stir-fry until the liquid has evaporated.
5. Add the vinegar, sesame oil, and green onion. Stir well and serve.

If no chicken stock is available, water may be substituted.

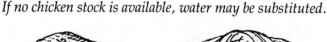

RECIPE INDEX

Appetizers

Beverages

Breads and Dumplings

Desserts and Dessert Accents

RECIPE INDEX

Entrées

Pasta, Rice and Vegetables

Salads and Salad Dressings

DINING IN–THE GREAT CITIES

A Collection of Gourmet Recipes from the Finest Chefs in the Country

---

Each book contains gourmet recipes for complete meals from the chefs of 21 great restaurants.

___ *Dining In–Baltimore*	7.95		___ *Dining In–St. Louis*	7.95
___ *Dining In–Boston*	7.95		___ *Dining In–San Francisco*	7.95
___ *Dining In–Chicago, Vol. II*	8.95		___ *Dining In–Seattle, Vol. II*	7.95
___ *Dining In–Dallas*	7.95		___ *Dining In–Sun Valley*	7.95
___ *Dining In–Denver*	7.95		___ *Dining In–Toronto*	7.95
___ *Dining In–Hawaii*	7.95		___ *Dining In–Vancouver*	8.95
___ *Dining In–Houston, Vol. I*	7.95		___ *Feasting In Atlanta*	7.95
___ *Dining In–Houston, Vol. II*	7.95		___ *Feasting In New Orleans*	7.95
___ *Dining In–Kansas City*	7.95			
___ *Dining In–Los Angeles*	7.95		**Forthcoming Titles —**	
___ *Dining In–Milwaukee*	7.95		___ *Dining In–Cleveland*	8.95
___ *Dining In–Minneapolis/St. Paul*	7.95		___ *Dining In–Manhattan*	8.95
___ *Dining In–Monterey Peninsula*	7.95		___ *Dining In–Philadelphia*	8.95
___ *Dining In–Pittsburgh*	7.95		___ *Dining In–Phoenix*	8.95
___ *Dining In–Portland*	7.95		___ *Dining In–Washington, D.C.*	8.95

☐ CHECK HERE IF YOU WOULD LIKE TO HAVE A
DIFFERENT DINING IN–COOKBOOK SENT TO YOU
ONCE A MONTH

Payable by MasterCard, Visa or C.O.D. Returnable if not satisfied.
List price plus $1.00 postage and handling for each book.

BILL TO:

Name _____

Address _____

City _____ State ____ Zip _____

SHIP TO:

Name _____

Address _____

City _____ State ____ Zip _____

☐ Payment enclosed ☐ Send C.O.D. ☐ Charge

Visa # _____ Exp. Date _____

MasterCard # _____ Exp. Date _____

Signature _____

PEANUT BUTTER PUBLISHING

2445 76th Avenue S.E. • Mercer Island, WA 98040
(206) 236-1982

CH 482

DINING IN–THE GREAT CITIES

A Collection of Gourmet Recipes from the Finest Chefs in the Country

Each book contains gourmet recipes for complete meals from the chefs of 21 great restaurants.

___ *Dining In–Baltimore*	7.95	___ *Dining In–St. Louis*	7.95
___ *Dining In–Boston*	7.95	___ *Dining In–San Francisco*	7.95
___ *Dining In–Chicago, Vol. II*	8.95	___ *Dining In–Seattle, Vol. II*	7.95
___ *Dining In–Dallas*	7.95	___ *Dining In–Sun Valley*	7.95
___ *Dining In–Denver*	7.95	___ *Dining In–Toronto*	7.95
___ *Dining In–Hawaii*	7.95	___ *Dining In–Vancouver*	8.95
___ *Dining In–Houston, Vol. I*	7.95	___ *Feasting In Atlanta*	7.95
___ *Dining In–Houston, Vol. II*	7.95	___ *Feasting In New Orleans*	7.95
___ *Dining In–Kansas City*	7.95		
___ *Dining In–Los Angeles*	7.95	**Forthcoming Titles —**	
___ *Dining In–Milwaukee*	7.95	___ *Dining In–Cleveland*	8.95
___ *Dining In–Minneapolis/St. Paul*	7.95	___ *Dining In–Manhattan*	8.95
___ *Dining In–Monterey Peninsula*	7.95	___ *Dining In–Philadelphia*	8.95
___ *Dining In–Pittsburgh*	7.95	___ *Dining In–Phoenix*	8.95
___ *Dining In–Portland*	7.95	___ *Dining In–Washington, D.C.*	8.95

☐ CHECK HERE IF YOU WOULD LIKE TO HAVE A
DIFFERENT DINING IN–COOKBOOK SENT TO YOU
ONCE A MONTH

Payable by MasterCard, Visa or C.O.D. Returnable if not satisfied.
List price plus $1.00 postage and handling for each book.

BILL TO: **SHIP TO:**

Name _____   Name _____

Address _____   Address _____

City _____ State ___ Zip ___   City _____ State ___ Zip ___

☐ Payment enclosed   ☐ Send C.O.D.   ☐ Charge

Visa # _____ Exp. Date _____

MasterCard # _____ Exp. Date _____

Signature _____

PEANUT BUTTER PUBLISHING
2445 76th Avenue S.E. • Mercer Island, WA 98040
(206) 236-1982

CH 482